My Credo

No Boundaries, No Conclusions

ROBERT L. MADDOX, JR.

© 2025
Published in the United States by Nurturing Faith, Macon, GA.
Nurturing Faith is a book imprint of Good Faith Media (goodfaithmedia.org).
Library of Congress Cataloging-in-Publication Data is available.

ISBN: 978-1-63528-259-7

All rights reserved. Printed in the United States of America.

Scripture quotations are from New Revised Standard Version Bible, copyright © 1989 National Council of the Churches of Christ in the United States of America. Used by permission. All rights reserved worldwide.

The views, thoughts, and opinions expressed are the author's own and do not represent the views of Good Faith Media and Nurturing Faith.

To Linda and our Fringer Friends

Contents

Acknowledgments 1
Welcome All Fringer Friends 3
Introduction 5
I AM a Creator without the Creator Person 15
I AM a Cumulative Christian Tradition Person 19
I AM a Three Fundamental Markers Person 21
I AM a Universe Person 25
I AM the Earth as Playing Field Person 31
Meet the Family: I Am a Genus Homo Person 35
I Am a Homo Sapiens Person 39
I Am a Secure Affirming Life-force Person 55
I Am a "That Something with No Boundaries and
    No Conclusions Happened 20-to-200 CE" Person 73
Yes, I Am a Jesus Person 85
I Am a Faithing Non-theist Cumulative Christian Tradition
    of the 21st Century Person 91
I Am a Hebrew Bible/Christian Testament Person 95
I Am an Ecclesia, Local Jesus Club, Person 105
The Author 109
Selected Bibliography 111

Acknowledgments

I am greatly indebted to several influential writings: *Genesis* by Guido Tonelli, *Humanimal* by Adam Rutherford, *Sapiens* by Yuval Noah Harari, *Spirit Wheel* by Steven Charleston, *Galileo* by James Reston Jr., *Einstein* by Walter Isaacson, *Why the Bible Began* by Jacob Wright, *Black Holes* by Brian Cox and Jeff Forshaw, *Unbelievable* by John Shelby Spong, *After Jesus Before Christianity* by Erin Vearcombe, Brandon Scott, and Hal Tausig, *Theopoetics* by Amos Wilder, *Acts and Christian Beginnings* by Dennis E. Smith and Joseph B. Tyson. Gratitude is also extended to Marcus Borg, Jon Dominic Crossan, and Elaine Pagels.

Boundless mind and spirit enrichment have come from Bill Rogers, Dan McGee, Maynard Moore, Tony Martin, Frank Harvey, Paul Bermingham, Tim Tutt, John Pierce, Sid Winters, and our three splendid children: Andy, Ben, and Elizabeth.

A tumultuous drumroll for Joy Hakim for helping me meet science again for the first time. And thanks to Pete Davis and John Pierce who, with skill and scholarship, provided professional editing.

A plea for patience: This book started out as a personal memoir, the product of years of reading, writing, talking with friends, attending seminars and conferences led by eminent biblical scholars. To my delight and honor, Nurturing Faith has again offered to help me by publishing my *Credo*. Thus, accurate attributions are not always precisely identified. I have made a serious effort to list every remembered source book in the bibliography. Thank you and thank sometime daunted editors.

Welcome All Fringer Friends

I would like to say a brief word
In support of the lunatic fringe.
At the edge of polite society
Where the really interesting people hang out.

I have met wild eyed dreamers, optimistic visionaries
Unrepentant seekers, and more than a few average folks
Who just like to think for themselves.

Out here there are no party lines to follow
No castes or outcasts, no gated communities of the heart
There are only envelopes to be pushed,
Barriers to be broken, and love to be risked.

I just want to say to all of my fellow fringers:
I am glad to have you out here with me.[1]

—Steven Charleston

Note

[1] Steven Charleston, *Spirit Wheel* (Minneapolis, Broadleaf Books, 2023), 85.

Introduction

This Jesus thing is finally not so complicated: Walk, talk, love, and serve others like Jesus and you're in, you get the Jesus button.

Being a Christian involves memory, history and story.[1]
—Diana Butler Bass

Let There Always Be Light
(Searching for Dark Matter)

Whatever they turn out to be,
Let there be swarms of them,
Enough for immortality,
Always a star where we can warm ourselves.
Let there be enough to bring it back
From its own edges
To bring us all so close we ignite
The bright spark of resurrection.[2]
—Rebecca Elson

Living and thinking on the edge was not a goal of mine, but that is what happened. For most of my thinking life, I have been a *fringer*. It is nice to have grand *fringer* companions.

Well into my ninth decade of life, my mortality clock ticks away. Before the cuckoo bird chirps her last call, I want to lay down my credo—*some fringer* benchmarks that frame my existence at this point. With these basic benchmarks, I meet "again for the first time" the universe, the Earth, genus *Homo*, and species *sapiens*.

Having settled where I live, and getting somewhat acquainted with my ancient kinfolk, perhaps you the reader of these "I am" confessions can join me the writer in meeting YHWH (God), Jesus, the

Hebrew Bible and the Christian Testament and Ecclesia in a fresh way.

We need poetry, desperately.[3]
   —Guido Tonelli

The venerable Amos Wilder (1895-1993) introduced me to the term theopoetic. Theology along with all great human endeavors must be framed by poetry and imagination. If the poetics fail, our great generative ideas become "ossified," dogmatic, devoid of elasticity.[4] Through these *I ams*—via theopoetics—maybe we can meet our ancestors and ourselves "again for the first time."

A close friend reminds me that much of what I lay out in this short memoir is far off the religious and personal track for most people. I knew that going in. Why, then make this effort? Two key words persist for me: honesty and liberation.

The serious, adventurous faithing walk that energizes me invites joyful, unremitting, beckoning honesty. Years ago, I began a conversation with myself as I reveled in the "whys and what ifs" of biblical religion. It steadily dawned on me that something as rich and all-embracing as this Jesus thing could stand up under my fumbling questioning. Thus, at this later life stage, I have marked my own place to stand. No, not really just standing. I do not simply rest here.

> **Why, then make this effort?**
> **Two key words persist for me:**
> **honesty and liberation.**

My wife Linda and I have a story from our young days at the gorgeous Ridgecrest Assembly, now long gone, near Asheville, North Carolina. A woman who had grown up in the Smokies spoke one day: "When I was young, standing on the porch with my father, I asked him, 'Daddy, what lies beyond those mountains?' He replied, 'Beyond those mountains are open doors.'"

Beyond my own version of faithing questions, the vision of open doors never ceases to tantalize me. With this credo in mind, I hope you will take flights of imagination with me and knock on your own faithing's closed doors. Amazing freedom and spiritual liberation are ours beyond those doors. So, let's knock on some new doors.

A trusted colleague of fifty years asked me where this *fringer* stuff came from. I have come to these places as a result of decades of wondering as I wander. Years of wondering have whetted my personal historical, biblical, and theological appetite to make a serious, consistent effort to get inside my faithing as a Jesus person Christian (the use of *faithing*: I employ, for me, a verb form *faithing* to emphasize faith as action, a way of living). I decided not to stop, to keep wondering as long as I am able to wander.

Beginning in some scary times as a Baptist boy of the early 1950s, enduring harrowing revival meetings and hard-hitting Youth for Christ rallies, nagging questions crept into my teenage brain.

For instance, an axial epiphany occurred to me in the spring of my freshman year at Baylor University during my first college religion course. Studying for an impending New Testament test, the question popped into my head: What does the resurrection of Jesus 2,000 years ago have to do with my life in 1956?

The answer popped just as clearly—nothing! Wow! That was spooky. I filed the moment away, maybe to unpack later. Obviously, the moment has stayed fresh in my head, and I am still unpacking that "Wow" moment.

In later years, with more academic equipment at hand, I started asking of the Way of Jesus the perfectly logical and credible five Ws—When, Where, What, Who, and Why. We engage in that interrogative exercise all the time with history, science, parenting, sexuality, sports, etc. As a truly serious Jesus person since adolescence, I decided along the way the Jesus way of life should not be exempt from these basic questions. This aborning adventure was far more than an academic trip. I genuinely wanted to get inside this Christianity thing that formed the basis of my life.

Understand, I am not a newcomer to this range of inquiry. I attended Sunday School since I could walk. As a teenager, I reveled in youth camps, attended revivals, and so-called Bible studies. As a seeking high school senior, I flirted briefly with the idea of attending the super fundamentalist Bob Jones University. With his rare univocal "No," my father nixed that notion. I was relieved.

Headed to ministry (Baptist, what else?) from age 19, I took most of the religion courses the university offered. Three years of seminary and five years of doctoral work gave me exposure to current (traditional) biblical and theological studies. The years of graduate work, especially one particular course at Emory University, played a major role in excising my faithing cataracts. The professor urged us to "encounter" ourselves in the sermon text before us. If we could not find ourselves in that passage, leave it. Move to another place that gripped us and return to it later. Watershed!

Still not enough. Not sufficient. I had a smattering of exposure to critical contemporary biblical scholarship that nudged me to keep moving. As a young pastor, I read the autobiography of Harry Emerson Fosdick where he rose up against my Baptist fundamentalism.

When John A.T. Robinson and his "God is dead" boutique theology erupted, I read into that genre. All the while, reluctant to go to seed on radical stuff, I devoured Keith Miller's *The Taste of New Wine* and every other book that Word Publishers produced. I genuinely wanted to know Jesus and that eventually pushed me to learn all I could about him and the Galilean world that enabled him.

In 1995, my journey led me to a mind-blowing, old/new fork in the road: **I met Jesus of Nazareth**. For me, after meeting the walking, talking Jesus through Marcus Borg and a host of warm and compelling scholars, women and men, I joined them in asking and find-

In 1995, my journey led me to a mind-blowing, old/new fork in the road: I met Jesus of Nazareth. ing fresh imaginative directions for the five Ws. Meeting Jesus of Nazareth "again for the first time" was scary when it dawned on me that Jesus was a man with a daily life not unlike the rest of us mortals.

Rather than tossing away decades of life as a Baptist Christian, I began carefully building on all those previous years of study and Southern Baptist culture (Southern Baptist financial support enabled me to attend seminary for $100.00 a semester). I embarked on a decidedly focused determination to find some personal, authentic faithing for me as a Jesus person.

Were those beckoning new places dependable? Trustworthy? Sustainable? Safe? It took more time and often unnerving study. Gradually, then with more assurance, I put my faithing weight down as mist surrounding Jesus and the five Ws gradually lifted.

For me, the five Ws are not just a fashionable, theological fruitcake of the second half of the twentieth century. From the get-go of the Jesus way, men and women asked those same questions. Actually, Jesus and Paul started the whole Ws thing for Christianity.

"Bring me children," Jesus said to a surprised crowd that sadly regarded children as laborers. Women and men could become his traveling companions. He offered healing to foreigners, even (gasp!) Romans. Peter would eat with Romans—at least some of the time. Adding a dash of credulity, the gospels remember a time when a persistent Gentile woman got Jesus to change his mind (Matthew 21:15-26). New followers of Jesus, now becoming the Christ (Anointed), did not need to keep kosher, Paul insisted. Jesus people in Galilee and on the North African Mediterranean coast, while acknowledging his death, began to sing that entering into Jesus' life was the path to full humanity.⁵

A cadre of Jesus women and men had the temerity to say one could go directly to God without the benefit of a priest—even under the leadership of women. In the Dark Ages, more than a few people were burned to death when they asked their own set of W questions.

Did I find definitive answers to my persistent questions? Yes and no. I opened a few previously closed or hidden doors. I concur that nothing is finally definitive. I also aver that unvarnished humility is a critical mindset for all human pursuits. What I am still uncovering makes personal, religious, and historical sense to me. I am here to report that my faithing remains strong and liberating as I have invested these extraordinary years on the Ws.

Don't be afraid. Reach out beyond what you grew up with. The Jesus way can handle our questions. Meet the historic and the twenty-first century. Discover the Matthew 25:34-40 Jesus again for the first time. You will be glad you did. In all this, I constantly remind myself that the "whole is greater than the sum of its parts."

Perhaps you are asking, "Where do I start my own fresh faithing journey?" Sad to say, your local clergy person will probably not be much help with the Ws. Far too many clergy across the board stopped serious study when they finished seminary, assuming all the serious W questions surfaced in seminary. Your local minister is also likely caught in the clutches of maintaining their own version of a not-for-profit business commonly called a church. They have decided not to rock their boats. Too often clergy are afraid to toss new-sounding ideas into the local church and cultural hopper.

On Sundays too often, our congregations get the same praise band music, prayers, and sermons year after year. As a starter, the preacher comes up with a clever opening joke, and here we go again. Whipped-up pop music and bland or frenzied, angry preaching stir up a hollow ecstasy devoid of transformative burning bush and Mount of Transfiguration awe. Amos Wilder in *Theopoetics* laments ginned up ecstasy when a penetrating openness to grand biblical moments can inspire genuine transcendence.[6]

If you have read this far, let's move on a bit. Get in a comfortable chair. I am on your side, a fellow pilgrim. That same good friend I mentioned earlier said my ideas in these pages threatened the "trees in his forest of faith." Leave those familiar trees in place. Just plant some new ones. Remember, I point you to a substantial bevy of likewise friendly, pilgrim *fringers* who are gifted biblical arborists. I listed some of my favorite books in the bibliography.

These *I Ams* are mine; these affirmations are for me and from me. Maybe, as your years go by, you can find some of them generative and/or frame some of your own. This Jesus thing is never done.

My dear friend's words echo, "Who is going to pay much attention to what you say?" My new mentors and I have established a community of *fringers*. For the past thirty years, a host of folks, young and not so young, and I have trekked this exciting road less traveled. Some of my favorite *fringer* scholars have sold millions of books and invited folks everywhere to meet Jesus of Nazareth again for the first time. So, you pay your money and take your choice as my sagacious mother-in-law reminded me. I find high adventure in writing, listening to willing readers, and revising my credo.

Venture out with me on a faithing journey rife with poetry and imagination—not fretting about boundaries and conclusions.

I am asking you to join me on this journey
I have no rules for you to follow if you come along.
To be honest, I don't even have a real idea
Where we are going.

In many ways, it is all a great mystery.
So think about my invitation
I don't want to convert you.
I want to amaze you.*[7]*

Behind all the laws of nature there remains something subtle, intangible, impenetrable. Veneration before this sense of awe and transcendence is my religion.[8]

—Albert Einstein

In these *I Ams*, I extend an invitation to open those heavy drapes around your mind, admitting bright sunshine. Travel with me into evolving realms of amazement. We humans are new on our wandering, wondrous planet. Dinosaurs ruled the planet from 200 million years to 65 million years ago when (current theory) an asteroid smacked us somewhere in Mexico setting up an atmospheric mass extinction for these creatures.

Humans began to emerge maybe a million years ago on our star that's at least three billion years old. We *sapiens* have an even shorter history, about 300,000 years. We made our first boats only 50,000 years ago. Dogs have been our best friend for only 30,000 years.

I can remember our first television set, the blessing of air conditioning, and the wonder of automatic transmissions in our cars. And here we are in the twenty-first century, still shaking the stardust from our sleepy eyes.

Let's decide that the amazement of stuff that really matters is yet with us. Let's be freshly astounded at ideas, new perspectives, enlarged hopes, and shared responsibilities. Let us unbind our imagination. As a starter, Guido Tonelli in his elegant book *Genesis: The Story of How Everything Began* reminds me that as rich as ancient creation myths are, the creation sagas that opened since Galileo in the sixteenth century are even more astounding and awe-inspiring.[9]

Notes

1. Diane Butler Bass, A People's *History of Christianity* (New York, HarperCollins, 2009), 9.
2. Rebecca Elson, "Let There Always Be Light," *The Universe in Verse*, Maria Popova (Massachusetts, Story Publishers, 2024) 35.
3. Guido Tonelli, Gene*sis: The Story of How Everything Began* (New York, Picador, 2019) 9.
4. Amos Wilder, *Theopoetic* (Oregon, WIPF & STOCK, 1972), 2.
5. Karen King, The Gos*pel of Mary Magdalene* (California, Polebridge Press, 2003), 155.
6. Wilder, *Theopoetic*, 66.
7. Charleston, *Spirit Wheel*, 120.
8. Walter Isaacson, *Einstein* (New York, Simon and Schuster, 2017), 88.
9. Tonelli, *Genesis*, 80.

I AM a Creator
without the Creator Person

It's my view that the simplest explanation is that there is no God. No one created the universe. No one directs our fate.[1]
—Stephen Hawking

For an opening *amazement*, from a long lifetime of wandering wonder in our universe, I have come to a fundamental assertion: we do not have a *Book-of-Genesis The Creator*, who from the edge of nowhere spoke into existence and/or directs all that we see and know, as well as what we do not yet see and know of the cosmos, our astounding planet, and each other.

This declaration both solves and generates serious questions. Stay with me for a while. Later, with help from Dr. Jacob Wright (*Why the Bible Began*), I will go into more intriguing details on the origin of the YHWH of Genesis and the timeless creation story that has shaped much of western cosmology, theology, and poetry for more than two thousand years.

Absent *The Creator*, we do have three billion years of effervescent, ever-emerging Life-force generated life forms on our planet. Evolution, marching to its own drumbeat, fed by a universe imbued with every element necessary for beginning, becoming, and continuing brought myriads of the stuff of life forms to infant Earth. The universe blessed us by birthing in the right place at the right time to incubate the multi-billion-year showers of stardust.

Over the passage of billions of cosmic electromagnetic ticks of what we call time, these life forms morphed into creatures capable of language, imagination, compassion, evil, creativity, reproduction, and no small measure of resilience.

As I suggest *no The Creator*, I am not casting us alone in the void to live, thrash around for three score and ten, and then die. In fact, we are not alone when we confront monumental questions without obvious answers. We subliminally or consciously call on each other, our religions, our collective reasoning, as well as the good and bad we have done with and for each other for eons. In short, we lay out the most enduring gift we can vouchsafe to one another—our million-year-old collective, connected, and generative *humanity*.

Charles Darwin (1809-1882) has convinced most of us that we benefit from a total connectivity with all life forms from the beginning through today. I translate Darwin's assertion to say we are generated by and within the un-generated, connected Life-force. I take a leap: as such, in 2025, we present our world and each other's untold treasures of conjoined heart, soul, mind and body. The Life-force that impregnated with no boundaries that "day with no yesterday"[2] generates, from and to each other, an astounding gift to every living creature in our uniquely-beginning home.

Paul Bermingham, one of my favorite *fringers*, reminds me that we humans have the creating gene. Since we oozed out of the oceans, we have never stopped creating on our home turf, our planet. For instance, Paul and his gifted wife Francois are creating a model organic farm fifty minutes from the White House. The two of them stood in awe recently as their favorite cow gave birth to a healthy, strapping, walking bull calf.

Choctaw Chief Charleston Steven sings:

We will walk together through the long stretch of road, all of us who have come this far into the valley of shadows. We will not be afraid or anxious for we have one another. We have our shared strength, our common wisdom, and our collective memory to help us through whatever may come. We have the quiet counsel of our elders and the boundless energy of our young ones. We have the depth of faith of many courageous hearts. We have the resilience *and experience of all those among us who have passed this way before and when the going gets hard, we have a thousand voices to sing, singing, as we go along the twisted path toward the higher ground, where the shadows will be far behind us.*³

She, the Spirit

*The opportunity of our time is that depth is again calling to depth.*⁴
—Amos Wilder

While I maintain my persuasion that the universe is self-generated and generating, I listen carefully to someone like indigenous elder Steven Charleston when he sings about the Spirit. For (Episcopal Bishop) Chief Steven, in keeping with the indigenous emphasis on the maternal, he regards the genderless Spirit through a feminine motif. *She* is the primordial *ruach* of Genesis, the Holy Spirit for Christians, the Great Spirit of Native Americans, YHWH of the Hebrews, Allah for the Muslims, Wisdom for Eastern faiths, and/or collective humanity for humanists.

Charleston intentionally leaves names and theologies for the individual. Spirit is neither theological nor dogmatic. Spirit is impenetrable yet completely accessible, without zip code but here for all who exercise faithing to climb out of the womb-like "kiva" into the light of hope and courage.⁵

*The spirit is not to be quenched and always welcomes our testing.*⁶
—Amos Wilder

For me, the Spirit is the collective *Us*, the *I don't know what's at the heart of the mystery*. Though not a Creator, she is our partner in creating. She almost never makes a big noise or leaves a visible footprint in the sands of our lives. She echoes the Big Bang though she did not pull the switch. I am not trying to make it easier to say *no The Creator*. I am bundling the whispers of millions of my fellow travelers who live within the ineffable mystery. The Spirit does not intrude nor

For me, the Spirit is the collective Us, the I don't know what's at the heart of the mystery. Though not a Creator, she is our partner in creating.

control anything yet is available always. Do I understand what I am saying? No, I do not understand. Is Spirit a product of wishful thinking? Maybe. Is she our DNA embedded in us from that "day without a yesterday?" Is she Big Bang, kinship, connectivity, unconditional love? Is she the essence of our humility when we existentially aver that pigs *may yet fly*? Perhaps.

Notes

[1] Stephen Hawking, from sources from a lecture in 2010.
[2] Georges Lemaitre, from many public sources. In 1927, Belgium physicist Georges Lemaitre introduced the theory that became the Big Bang as a way to describe the origin of the universe.
[3] Steven Charleston, *The Ladder of Light* (Minneapolis, Broadleaf Books, 2021), 75.
[4] Wilder, *Theopoetic*, p. 21
[5] Charleston, *Ladder of Light*, 10.
[6] Wilder, *Theopoetic*, 22.

I AM a Cumulative Christian Tradition Person

Harvard University's Dr. Cantwell Smith (*The Meaning and End of Religion*), rang a resounding bell for me when he chimed that we live within eons of "cumulative (human) traditions."[1]

Tradition is not static even though we sometimes allow ourselves to get stuck in a non-productive "idolatrous traditionalism"[2] ethos. We swim in this ever-flowing river of evolving, expanding cumulative traditions. I build on traditions handed to me by parents, grandparents, Martin Luther King Jr., Gandhi, Abraham Lincoln, Jesus, and more. Through faithing birthed by traditions we can live the abundant life Jesus promised those who open themselves to the ways of caring for others as we want others to care for us. As we move along, I will talk more about this pivotal, generative axiom.

Bona fides

These *I Ams* come from me after seventy years of life-shaping, serious, fun, energizing, widespread reading, study, and respectful listening with no small measure of humility kneaded into the dough. No, I am not trying to be contrarian, nor am I breaking new ground except for myself. Others have nurtured these thoughts long before me. My years of *I Am-ing* have unfolded productively by the energy of a beckoning curiosity.

Notes

[1] Wilfred Cantwell Smith, *The Meaning and End of Religion* (Princeton, Princeton University Press, 1972), 101ff.

[2] Stuart Higginbotham, *The Heart of a Calling* (New York, The Crossroad Publishing Company, 2021), 7.

I AM a Three Fundamental Markers Person

These are restless ambiguity, existential confidence, and a life of faithing.

Restless ambiguity

Restless ambiguity means my mind churns with ferment, stirring around on ideas, questions, and directions that are new or resurfaced to me. Excessive ambiguity has not bothered me for a long time. I am not always sure about myself, who I am, where I should be going, or how I should be relating to loved ones. Still, I have managed these *I Ams* with reasonable equanimity, now approaching nine decades with them tossing around in my head. My ambiguities do not threaten life as we know it. I do not have to wonder how to manage a pandemic, China, Donald Trump, or the national debt. Still my ambiguities persist, real in my life. I can live with what I know with workable certainty and what I know of what I don't know. My ambiguities tend to keep me mentally and spiritually charged up. Thus, I am not afraid of ambiguity.

Existential confidence

I have been gifted with a good measure of existential confidence. I do not think of this measure of confidence with a smug attitude. My parents, Bob and Virginia Maddox, faced their lives as newlyweds of the Great Depression, soon with a family of four sons caught up in the whirling vortex of World War II and beyond. They managed with confidence, spoken and lived, with steady *"Yes, we can do this."* I never knew them to look back with much "woe is me" groaning. I do not regard my parents as reflective, especially on the larger issues of life. My parents in their easy not-knowing gave me the freedom to look for my own knowing. Bob and Virginia would not recognize much of my knowing at 88, but they would both love me still and fry two chickens for Sunday lunch.

In addition to my birth, my measure of existential confidence may well be their most important gift to me. This sense of confidence imbues me with an unadorned peace in facing life and death. My father would often remind me that everyone steps into their pants just like I do, one leg at a time. Presidents, kings, and potentates must eat, sleep, dress, use the bathroom every day, and look around at the world in which we live. And we know that nearly all of us like sex and reproduction: we all get here in the same way. In my life, I have met three US presidents, billionaires, great writers, humanitarians, and thousands of folks like you and me. I can appreciate achievement and genius but not for a long time have I been intimidated by folks with more stuff than I possess. Many people are much smarter than I am. At the same time, I am much smarter than many other people. I have worked hard to be smart, but I did not do this by myself.

Linda, professors, books, farmers, schoolteachers, Uber drivers, and restaurant servers have shared their wisdom with me. My gratitude goes to all these known and unknown sages; hence, existential confidence. I owe a special thanks to Dorothy Cook, my late mother-in-law from Thomaston, by way of tiny Whigham, in deep southern Georgia. Dorothy was the most courageous social activist and lay theologian anywhere. With grace, humor, and insight she had wisdom for any occasion: "You step on your toe to stop the toothache." "Things without remedy are things without regard." "You can't make jelly in the kitchen while rocking on the front porch." When I puzzled over the salvation of people in Africa who had never heard of Jesus, she pulled up her biblical sagacity to assure me that, "God will take care of them." She read every book I studied in seminary.

Faithing

I have lived an imperfect life of faithing. Faithing as praxis can be generated and augmented by one's religious outlook. Faithing can be appropriated by burnishing genetic and DNA givens. Faithing can be undergirded by connecting with similarly motivated people. Faithing is hope, commitment, trust, praxis. These are tethered to, embraced by, and infused with a sense of assurance that cosmic order exists the way it should. Faithing becomes richer when laced with education, poetry, imagination, and openness to fresh breezes. Not precise. Not manipulative. Not given to neat definition but workable and sustaining.

My iteration of faithing underpins my basic sense of confidence. Can I get rattled? Of course. Usually, however, the rattling doesn't last long. The overall stability of my life with Linda Cook Maddox remains an undeniable, invigorating source of yes-ness. Our inevitable, unique to us, ups and downs, have marked our sixty-five years together and keep us connected though these latter years have taken us to new places. We are gifted with three outstanding children, and a splendid extended family and dear friends.

Faithing is not the absence of critical thought
But thought put to the greatest questions.
We were made to reason to wonder to ask
For only by these gifts do we discover
The far reaches of the Spirit's imagination.
Religion is not a court but a laboratory.
We were not made to conform, but to explore
Every doubt may be a door.[1]

Faithing is a life journey into the unknowable with no boundaries and no conclusions. It's like *pi*: real and workable while stretching beyond infinity. Nearly every human has some version of a cell phone. I would rather go outside without my shoes than leave my smartphone on the desk. These indispensable gadgets are, by design, ever new.

In this rapidly changing, tech-savvy world, let's get serious about our basic faithing perspective. A verse in Hebrews (13:8) sings, "Jesus Christ is the same yesterday and today and forever." Such a declaration may provide a measure of security, but it's not accurate. From the beginning of the Jesus movement we, his followers, have written, argued, theorized, and constantly updated our understanding of him. To this day, nothing about Jesus stays settled or final. He was in the same faithing boat as us as he sought to make plain the ways of Adonai in his own time.

Three assertions provide confidence and peace as I say there is *no The Creator*. Thus equipped, I continue to sail on the sea of faithing in my cobbled together but sturdy craft, navigating bravely with unseen but present companions toward Ithaca's lovely, inviting shores.

I am an old man getting younger.
The younger I become the more I want to play
Just a little longer
Before I hear my Father call
Before I have to sleep.[2]
　—Steven Charleston

Notes

[1] Charleston, *Spirit Wheel*, 141.
[2] Ibid, 24.

I AM a Universe Person

I was born 13.5 billion years ago. My Big Bang singularity Father inseminated the process. My Mother Earth endured the birth pangs. Father Universe and Mother Earth gave me sustenance as I struggled from blob to human. Hence, I am a universe person, residing for now in the bosom of Mother Earth. This is where I live and where I will die but never go away. Let us get better acquainted with both our celestial and earthly connections.

Cosmic calendaring is anything but settled. Take your pick.

The universe was created out of the particle-filled void.[1]

The Big Bang, a day without a yesterday.[2]

For cosmic theology there is no realm of experience in which we have been more out of touch than new categories of our modern vision of the creation. It is at the level of a theopoetic that these contemporary issues can be rightly explored.[3]

I offer these upcoming sketches of evolution, cosmology, and anthropology for my own amazement. I did poorly in college chemistry, eked out a passing grade in biology, and chalked up a decent grade in physics for dummies. What I offer here are peeks, "golly gee whizzes," gleanings from the past two years of fun yet serious study. So, skip through immeasurable eons with me. The vast (an adjective nowhere big enough to embrace what we know is "there" and what we know we do not know is "there," but is about the best linguistic tool I have) universe is littered with zillions of pieces of weighable, measurable pieces of matter. Our Earth, likewise, is a measurable piece of generally life-friendly matter. I revel in the imaginative poetry and music we have employed for millennia invariably magnificently, to celebrate the wonders of the universe. But more, particularly in my sunset years, I invest joyful hours to enrich my wondering in this stupendous wandering cosmos.

In my focus on the universe, rather than ponder theology, I have donned the mantle of a novice student of science. I heartily thank a new brilliant friend, Dr. Joy Hakim, for blessing thousands of us with her three books, *The Story of Science*—built around Aristotle, Isaac Newton, and Albert Einstein. Her books and related study generated by them have opened new worlds for me and nudged me into this *Credo* thing. In addition to the materiality of the universe, Joy's books, especially the one built around Albert Einstein, helped me draw open the universe's curtain a bit to get a glance at energy and light as fundamental ingredients of our universe. Einstein, in ways far beyond me, gave us $E=MC^2$, **E** Energy equals **M** mass times **C** the speed of light squared.[4]

From my teenage years, I began to encounter the language of evolution. I do not know where I picked that up. No one at my 1950s Georgia high school used the word. If our preachers said the word, it was disparaging. We did not talk about such notions at home around the dinner table. Nevertheless, I began to puzzle over evolution. I admit I did not engage in a profound, serious study of the question. Still the concept and the possibility stayed with me.

Of course, as a Baptist boy constantly exposed to Bible teachings, particularly of the genre that left no room whatsoever for questioning God's verbally-inspired word, I had my share of "What if?" questions. Revival preachers who came to our Baptist church had a way of saying about the Bible, "Believe all of it or none of it!" By about the ninth grade that screed did not fit well with me. I just had nothing in my faithing quiver with which to counter it.

How to mesh a "beginning" 13.5 billion years ago, millions and millions of years of evolution, dinosaurs, and early humans walking upright on two legs, and cave-dwelling artists with the six days of creation in Genesis and the preaching and teaching in church? I had no one to talk with about my burgeoning concerns.

Since ambiguity did not seriously bother me, I filed away the questions into a corner of my teenage brain with an existential confidence that, in time, faithing would help me work it out. Years have sped by. Thanks to much reading and listening, I found sufficient personal religious security to craft a workable way to regard the Genesis texts as echoes of time-honored campfire poetry and imagery. Hebrew scribes, for a variety of reasons, gave us YHWH, *The Creator*, about 2,500 years ago. Ancestral shamans sang their sagas generation to generation, possessed by the gift of wonder and imagination as they wandered. They lyrically chanted, danced, and sang on wings from their poetry-infused souls. Guido Tonelli in *Genesis* opines that at a distant moment in our primordial past some unknown ancestor "told a story" aimed at the questions that naturally arose among them sitting beneath the gorgeous night sky. Our ancestors did their best to tell timeless stories that helped them manage the heavens, creating in the process their "symbolic universe."[5] Their fables and sagas we still recite. I am grateful that I live in a time when I can comfortably adorn the campfire stories with breathtaking, ever-unfolding science.

A Timeline

Note: In terms of a timeline that brings us to the twenty-first century, I am dependent on a variety of credible books to construct this broad trajectory. Cosmological science speaks in terms of billions and multiplied millions of our years. When it comes to vast distances, science likewise measures in terms of millions of light years based on the speed of light generally calculated to travel at the rate of 186,000 miles per second in a vacuum. We earthlings calibrate our calculations in terms of years in a universe that couldn't care less about our puny calendar constructions.

Georges Lamaitre postulated the Big Bang in 1927. This moment beyond moments, this "today with no yesterday," either of gargantuan proportions or infinitesimally small, instantaneously exploded (to the minus hundreds of seconds), scattering massive clouds of wondrously generative matter into the vast, beyond measure, cosmic darkness. Over the course of billions of years, those protons and electrons of magnetically charged bits of matter began to coalesce into galaxies of millions of celestial bodies and stars beyond number. Among the several books I have explored, one favorite is *Genesis: The Story of How it All Began* by Guido Tonelli, an elegantly written treatise. The author wants to make serious cosmological science more understandable to non-scientists. But even after rereading, I miss much of the technical material. I did get a glimpse of Tonelli's big picture and the big calendar. His astounding narrative uses the biblical motif of "seven days" to guide us through the billions of years that brings us to the twenty-first century. The book is worth the effort.

Tonelli says the sun was on its way to formation about 3.5 billion years ago as cosmic matter uniquely coalesced around a particular primitive celestial body. Our solar system seems to be in a prolonged and reasonably stable place even as it expands with the rest of the universe. Beyond our solar system, our galaxy, the Milky Way is anything but still and quiet. Beyond our Milky Way, astronomers are discovering an endless cacophony of universes.

Astronomical news postulates that at the center of our galaxy and throughout the universe boils and bubbles devouring black holes, the gargantuan residues of dying stars. With the enormous gravitational pull of countless black holes, our universe is steadily being drawn into the vortex generated by the black holes. Tonelli in *Genesis* says we need not be overly anxious about our fate. It would take millions of years for our solar system to be sucked into a black hole. Eons of constant cosmic showers have brought Earth essential life-generating elements initially scattered exponentially from the Big Bang and the ever-expanding universe.

The laws of probability and possibility underpin the theory that ours is not the only body so fortuitously blessed in a galactic system of billions of possibilities. So far, however, even with the astounding probing telescopes and sophisticated mathematical equations, we earthlings have not found another life-giving celestial nursery like ours.

At some point in our planet's infancy, a wandering, lonely cosmic body with a diameter of 3,000 km slammed into baby Earth and attached itself for an immeasurable number of eons. Gratefully, the collision apparently did little damage to either body. In cosmic time, that body gradually separated from the Earth, floated 250,000 miles from us and became our moon. The configuration and location of the moon appears to be unique in the known universe in its relationship to the Earth. The moon plays an essential role in the evolution and stability of our planet. Without the reciprocal gravitational force of the moon to Earth and Earth to moon we would not have seasons and tides. In fact, we probably would not exist.

Thankfully another serendipitous piece of good cosmic fortune for our rocky planet is the fortuitous location of the gigantic planet Jupiter in relation to Earth. Along with other celestial bodies, with its gravitational strength, Jupiter forms a protective shield for Earth guarding against catastrophic collisions of roaming asteroids. Sixty-five million years ago, one incoming massive invader apparently did get through Jupiter's gravitational shield with cataclysmic results. More on that later.

At the risk of contradicting myself, while possibly being *pulled* into a black hole, the universe is still *expanding* at an astounding rate by earthly measurements. I have settled on a beautiful mantra: "We live in a wandering universe on a wandering planet." I thank an expanding field of knowledge, steadily amassed by an amazing host of women and men scientists. They continue to use their gifted minds and years of preparation and study to create bewildering mathematical equations, machines and satellites that will enable us steadily to understand more of the universe in which we live. So, here we are in our wondering as we live in a wandering universe on a wandering star.

Einstein Could Not Decide

An unsettled penultimate question swirls around the debate among great thinkers: does the universe continue on its journey of evolutionary creation by immutable laws encoded in nature, built into the very warp and woof of the process? Or does the universe's journey accommodate a measure of chance? Albert Einstein went to his grave looking for the unifying field theory that fully explained and managed the universe. He admitted that he never got there while insisting that the "Lord does not throw dice," that the universe continues on its way in terms of immutable, if more yet to be discovered, built-in laws of nature. Other scientists, like Max Planck, likewise of great brilliance, have maintained statistical room for chance, the science of quantum mechanics. This debate is way beyond my paygrade. Still, we need to know that the issue of the ways of nature being discovered or created is not settled.

Notes

[1] Tonelli, *Genesis*, 1.

[2] From the teachings of Georges Lemaitre.

[3] Wilder, *Theopoetic*, 5ff.

[4] Joy Hakim, *The Story of Science: Einstein Adds a New Dimension* (Washington, DC, Smithsonian Books, 2007), 190. Joy Hakim is not a scientist, rather she is a gifted writer with infinite curiosity, who offers three acclaimed books on the *Story of Science*.

[5] Tonelli, *Genesis*, 202-203.

I AM the Earth
as Playing Field Person

The earth is holy. She is our sacred mother.
Our mother needs us, calls to us.
Let every son and daughter stand up now
For what must be done to save her.[1]

Our speck of matter emerged at the right place at the right time some three billion years ago to reap the benefits of a universe laden with generative star dust.[2]

Choctaw Chief Steven remembers: My ancestors said the sun is the fire kindled before time began, the Earth is the hearth of that fire, and its light is life, scattered like embers into the night.[3]

Another song to sing: *If the universe is my father, the Earth is my mother. I learned to walk, talk, and think here thanks to the abiding care of my Mother Earth. Like most children, it has taken me a long time to more fully appreciate and adore my mother and to return love and care to her.*

Earth has served as host to life of one form or another for most of our planet's existence, upwards of three billion years.

Our earth is a measurable piece of generally life-friendly matter. All life on Earth is connected by common ancestry and that includes us. We humans who inhabit Earth are mobile, thinking, reproducing pieces of matter. Thus, we are part of a material universe in which a material Earth is tolerated at least for the next few million years. Today the spinning, vibrant Earth has water and food enough for seven billion of us material human creatures and a few billion more life forms. Matter, matter everywhere. Is that all? I really do not know what the more is. We humans emphatically intuit more. As I talk about the universe and Earth, I make room in my thinking and faithing for the unknowable more.

Four Principles Frame All Life Forms

I simply list these, but bow before their complexity. Someone else is more than welcome to give them a go.

- universal genetics,
- cell theory
- chromosomes
- evolution[4]

Cosmic Serendipity

Earth grew from the "inside" out. Elements from the eons of celestial bombardment from the universe formed what became the molten inner core of our planet. Layer after layer of generative matter poured in steadily to form enormous tectonic plates upon which the thin deposit of element-rich dirt formed where we live. Not to be bound to the Earth's innards and surfaces, yet more cosmic quantum waves gifted our planet with a thin but essential breathable atmosphere. That's the atmosphere today under assiduous assault by our carbon emissions.

For immeasurable ages, vast oceans have covered much of Earth. One source of oceanic water came as the universe showered our tiny aborning planet with ingredients that, over millions of years, could morph into water-producing vapors. Additionally, for years scientists have known that immense deposits of ice exist on rocky bodies like ours throughout the frigid universe. When time was irrelevant, cosmic forces combined to ensconce these enormous deposits of ice on wandering bodies including our fledgling planet. As immeasurable time flowed, our gutsy planet gained sufficient balanced gravitational relationship with the sun to become warm without being so close that we were torched. Gradual warming temperatures slowly melted the mountains of ice watering the planet with vast, eventually life-rich oceans. Likewise, heaving subterranean forces began to push volcanoes, towering mountains, and deep valleys up from the oceans' floors.

Thanks to those cascading showers of rich elements into the oceans, about a billion years ago tiny life forms began to generate in the stardust rich waters. Eventually, untold waves of these infinitely minuscule lifeforms connected. Then some gradually made their way out of the oceans to spaces that had dried out as seas and Earth reconfigured into regions of dry land.

Bone Creep

One astounding evolutionary event leads to another. About 530 million years ago, vertebrates began to form in the oceans. They were the product of development as single-cell organisms gradually attached to other single cell bodies. Over an infinitely long period of time, these single cells connected sufficiently to introduce the vertebrates into the ocean. Fish began to appear.

Two hundred million years ago, evolution began to go into overdrive to produce the fearsome reptiles that owned the planet. Throughout our long history, the Earth has experienced a series of disastrous mass extinctions. Invariably, however, from the consequences of these huge extinctions other life forms emerged to take up the spaces vacated by these changes. We will see more of this phenomenon for good or ill throughout history.

Such a mass extinction occurred 65 million years ago when that Greyhound bus-sized asteroid managed to get through Jupiter's protective shield. This intruder hit the Earth with a nuclear-like force. The world-wide dust clouds the invader unleashed brought about sufficient climate change that the Jurassic Park reptiles could not long survive. The extinction of the gigantic reptiles made a way for smaller animals to gain their footing and begin to thrive, including in a few more millions of years, our primate ancestors. Untold millions of these giants, buried under 65 million years of precious dirt have now come back from their graves with torrents of good news and bad news to feed the planet's voracious appetite for fossil fuels. If the giants posed a threat to the smaller creatures 150 million years ago, their remains are at it again in our era.

Scientists of the earth and heavens predict that our planet will ultimately go away in the inevitable sweep of the universe. They do hold out a future for us of several million years. In this twenty-first century of our reckoning, we have more than enough lethal power coupled with greed and indifference to do the universe's job of implosion.

Notes

[1] Charleston, *Spirit Wheel*, 41.
[2] Paraphrase from Tonelli, as well as my book *Genesis*.
[3] Charleston, *Ladder of Light*, 140.
[4] Adam Rutherford, *Humanimal* (United Kingdom, Weldenfield & Nicoloson, 2018), 23.

Meet the Family:
I Am a Genus Homo Person

I am greatly indebted to Adam Rutherford and Uval Harai for the substance of my synthesis of what follows.

"What a piece of work is man!" Hamlet intones, "...How like a God! The beauty of the world! The paragon of animals!"[1]
—William Shakespeare

We are an animal of no significance.[2]
—Noah Harari

Scientists divide creatures into genus and species. Our genus is *Homo* meaning man. Our species is *sapiens* meaning wise. Our genus *Homo* is more than three million years old. Genera are grouped into families. Individual families trace their lineage back to a founding matriarch.

Face it, we genus *Homo* humans are animals, members of a large and noisy family called the "great apes." A theory opines that six million years ago a primitive female primate birthed two daughters. One is the mother of today's chimpanzees. The other daughter is the mother of creatures who evolved into the genus *Homo*.

The total genus *Homo* story is quite complicated and debated among scientists. I am gathering up what I understand of *Homo*'s significant diversity under the taxonomy genus *Homo*. A more complete search would be fascinating but not for me at this point in my overcrowded brain.

Earth had humans before there was history. Humans resembling us emerged about 2.5 million years ago. Compared to the Big Bang 13+ billion years ago, humans are late players in the evolutionary drama. Those African humans would not have regarded themselves as special nor would it have crossed their minds that someday their progeny would rule the world.

Homo DNA is no different from anything that has lived in the last three million years. The coding system employed within the DNA is no different either. The four coded letters that make up DNA are the same in bacteria, bonobos, oats, bedbugs, barnacles, and Triceratops.

All life forms are organized into discrete cells. It's also universal science that these incalculably numerous cells harvest energy from the rest of the universe in a process common to all life forms.

About two million years ago, a significant number of these African *Homo* humans spread out to other parts of the planet. The various environments into which the groups moved gradually triggered/incorporated evolutionary changes to allow the groups to adapt to their environment. Thus, in Ice Age Europe, *Homo* Neanderthals grew larger and bulkier, enabling them to resist the persistent cold. The same nature of change occurred with other groups of humans depending on their environment.

Genus *Homo* walks on two legs. This takes more energy and fosters backache and muscle ache. Walking upright takes an additional toll on women. Walking upright narrows women's hips constricting the birth canal making childbirth painful and more dangerous.

For the first two million years of the existence of *Homo*, humans were fearfully subjected to predators. They ate far down the food chain, mainly the marrow from bones leftover from animals that had been killed and devoured by larger carnivores. Humans had to wait around until the lions and jackals had their fill. Resilient genus *Homo* learned to hold rocks and clubs as tools with their remarkable hands to crack open the bones.

Sexuality

From the beginning, Earth's life forms are heterosexual and homosexual. Before we knew about marrow as food, tools to crack open the marrow-rich bones, skins to keep warm, or fire for cooking, Earth's animals engaged in the power and pleasure of sex. Sexuality was not invented. It is part and parcel of every life form including us animals of many species. Sex, not Helen's face, launched the fabled thousand ships.

Certainly, many animals enjoy sex for pleasure and not just for procreation. Sexual encounter, penetration, and fertilization are timeless acts we humans continue to enjoy regardless of sexual orientation. For example, homosexual touching dominates male giraffes' sexual encounters.[3]

The fundamental purpose of sex is to make babies. Fact-checking however, paints a more nuanced picture. The statistician David Spieghalterin has puzzled out numbers for the sex lives of British people. Of every 1,000 sexual acts that could result in a baby, by choice only one encounter actually results in pregnancy. He estimates that something like 900 million acts of sexual activity take place every year in Britain alone, or roughly 100,000 per hour. If one extrapolates that to the seven billion humans alive on the Earth, it works out to be around 166,667 sexual acts that occur every minute. We are all somewhere on the fluidity of that sexuality spectrum.[4]

Compared to other animals, human babies are born prematurely. The colt can walk within a few minutes after its birth. The human baby is dependent on its elders for years. Raising a human baby takes a village. Evolution has favored the development of community and family as part of raising a child. Children thus born dependent on elders for years can also mean human children learn more skills from seniors.

Time and Evolution Marched On

Thanks to expanding language and subsequent improved communication, humans began to hunt larger animals 400,000 years ago. Going after bigger game such as elephants and bears required leadership, planning, coordination, and communication, hence culture was augmented by hunger and language.

Evolution, keeping pace with the environment, gifted humans with dexterous and skillful hands. Primates benefiting from a combination of random evolution and environmental demands, began to use their hands to make tools that extended their efficiency in foraging for food. These tools may be, at first, no more than sticks selected to enable them to stir grubs from inside of trees or higher up on limbs as they foraged for food. Within a few thousand more years they learned to craft axes and arrowheads from rocks.

One of our earliest genus cousins is named *Homo habilis* literally translating to "handyman." They lived in east Africa between 2.1 and 1.5 million years ago. They had long arms and small heads. Their brains were typically half the size of ours. Their handyman status is largely due to the discovery of lithic specimens, early stone technology. Rock specimens and flakes indicate a tool, particularly an ax type of tool chipped from a stone.

These actions imply a cognitive ability that enables a selection of suitable stones including a plan for shaping. *Homo habilis* is among the earliest members of our lineage that anthropologists have described as human; tool use is part of that definition.

In short, from two million years ago to 10,000 years ago, the Earth was home to a number of human species. *Homo sapiens* in no way had the planet to themselves. Stay tuned.

Notes

[1] William Shakespeare, as cited in Rutherford, *Humanimal*, 80.
[2] Noah Harari, *Sapiens*, HarperCollins, 2015, 4.
[3] Rutherford, *Humanimal*, 80.
[4] Rutherford, *Humanimal*, 80.

I Am a *Homo Sapiens* Person

One moon-lit night, my grandfather of a hundred thousand generations ago, flung his arms and eyes upward and exulted to that lunar man smiling back at him: I can talk! I can think! I can imagine. And I can paint my feelings on the walls of the caves where I live.[1]

Yes,
I am a card-carrying human being
I am not a political party, a denomination,
A class, a race, or a demographic.
I am just a human being.

I like to do what human beings like to do;
Live at peace, enjoy my life, be with the family.
I like learning from other human beings,

Sharing my own thoughts
And finding ways to make this world safer, happier,
And as natural as we can.
I am a card-carrying human being.[2]
　—Steven Charleston

The story of the Big Bang is called physics. The story of the way atoms and matter created molecules is called chemistry. The story of the way molecules created organisms is called biology. By about 300,000 years ago these primordial organisms had grown into a species of humans called Homo sapiens. This johnny-come-late species began to organize in such a way as to create culture. The story of culture is history. History touts that by 10,000 years ago, Homo sapiens were the only humans left on Earth. It's a great, sweeping story, our story.[3]

Until recently, we *Homo sapiens* regarded ourselves as unique, special, set apart, the ultimate crown of creation. Modern evolutionary, anthropological, and archeological science have revealed that sense of uniqueness to be a campfire story generated by ancestral shamans who sang only about what they knew.

Uval Harari in *Sapiens* says three revolutions shaped our *Homo sapiens*' history:

- The first of these began about 70,000 years ago, the cognitive revolution.
- The second is the agricultural revolution that got underway 12,000 years ago.
- The third is the scientific revolution that began only 500 years ago. The scientific Uvari revolution may end history and/or create something entirely new on the planet.[4]

Physically, our bodies are not drastically different from *Homo sapiens* in Africa from 200,000 years ago. We were then physically capable of speaking as we do today; our brains were not significantly different in size. Our genes have responded in small part to changes in the environment and diet. These genetic variants account for the minuscule percentage of DNA that spells out the difference between individuals in the most superficial characteristics of skin color, hair texture and a few others.

Sapiens in Charge

For the last 10,000 years, we *Homo sapiens* regarded ourselves as the only humans as, indeed, we are now. But we have cousins galore among the gorilla, chimpanzee, and orangutan families. We also have had brothers and sisters who no longer exist. What happened to them remains one of the unsolved mysteries, even secrets, of our time.

Communication skills and more lethal hunting tools enabled *Homo sapiens* 100,000 years ago to rise to the top of the food chain. These rapid skills jumps wrought enormous consequences.

Homo sapiens ate better by killing more of the tasty animals. Lions and sharks made it to the top of the food chain over millions of years giving the ecosystem time to adjust and to limit how much havoc the predators could wreak. *Sapiens'* rapid rise gave neither themselves nor the ecosystem adequate time to adjust to the increased demands. Scrambling vigorously for first place at the table generated creativity. The race for the top also fostered greed and fears among *sapiens* that likewise made us prone to be more intolerant, cruel, and selfish.

Homo sapiens have the largest brain among the animals in proportion to overall body weight. We do not know why evolution gave *Homo sapiens* a bigger brain. Perhaps evolution prompted *sapiens* to exchange brawn for brain? But having a large brain does not necessarily mean that more is better. Jumbo brains are a jumbo drain on the body. *Sapiens'* large brains require 25% of bodily energy consumption.[5]

For one reason or another, *Homo erectus* and all of the other genera *Homo* steadily disappeared. That left only *Homo sapiens* on the Earth. Why *Homo sapiens* and not another species? No one knows. One theory is that something genetically occurred, between 70,000 and 40,000 BCE, in the collective brain of those *sapiens* during the intervening millennia that set them on the path to become the only genus *Homo* on the Earth. Pure chance.[6]

For instance, Neanderthals, so named because of their discovery in the Neander River Valley, populated the then Ice Age climate of Europe in today's Germany. As *Homo sapiens* moved into their territory the Neanderthals steadily disappeared. Did *Homo sapiens* interbreed? Perhaps yes to a limited degree, but the family members were too different from each other for much interbreeding. Were *Homo sapiens* better hunters and gatherers, gradually starving their brothers and sisters to extinction? Or was it horrific genocide? We *Homo sapiens* have shown an ability and capacity to commit genocide.[7]

About 100,000 years ago, a band of *Homo sapiens* migrated from Africa to the Middle East. They failed to thrive and eventually moved back to east Africa. Scientists have speculated that this wave of *Homo sapiens* did not have the cognitive ability to manage their new environment. Then 70,000 years ago a second band of *Homo sapiens* migrated out of Africa. This time they successfully adapted to new environments. The 30,000-year interlude enabled a significant leap forward. This newly minted band of *Homo sapiens*, during those 30,000 years of fundamental refiguring, had learned to build boats, make oil lamps, bows and arrows, needles for sewing, and devise a measure of social stratification. In those 30,000 years, *Homo sapiens* had reached cognitive ability comparable to ours today.

Archaeology indicates that Neanderthals and *Erectus* hunted in small groups, maybe single families. The "new" *sapiens*, for instance, could forge a cooperative effort to round up herds of wild horses and spook them into blind canyons. Then, in a frenzy, they would kill, butcher, skin, and smoke the meat for preservation. This huge, bloody enterprise would likely not have been achieved by Neanderthals given their culture of solo and small group hunting.

Sapiens Learns to Think as Well as Talk

How did *sapiens* conquer our world? The secret, if it is a secret, is language. Language may well be the most important legacy of the cognitive revolution.[8] What was so special about the language that emerged during those 30,000 years? What sets them apart? They learned to use language for *symbolic communication*.[9] Other animals have language. A band of chimpanzees can warn one another that a lion is nearby. A matriarchal elephant can sound the way to water. Ground squirrels can notify others that an eagle is circling above them. Whales communicate through the ocean currents. Our language is subtle. We can convey infinite emotions. We can talk about, use, and store mountains of information. Can non-humans communicate subtly? Maybe. Our language evolved as a way to tell stories, share knowledge, and gossip about one another. And even more, our language can verbalize ideas, vividly describe that which does not appear to our eyes, and sense perception that had no corporeal identity. The chimp sees the lion and sends out an alarm. Groups and tribes among us communicate that the lion who is about to devour a gazelle he has brought down is actually the god of their tribe. If enough members of the tribe agree that the lion is their god it does not matter that they cannot see the deity represented by the lion. The lion becomes the tribe's god to whom they give allegiance, worship, and offer sacrificial food and sometimes, tragically, living members of the tribe.[10]

For thousands of years, *Homo sapiens* have used language to cast that which does not corporeally exist. On this *sapiens* evolutionary axis, imagination and poetry began to play a larger role in our development. Enriched by imagination and poetry, we *sapiens* created art, literature, religions, kingdoms, corporations, and nations built, by and large, on non-physical existence.

Theopoetic narratives emerged as generational stories to connect families and tribes to one another. If enough people in the given community agree with the sacerdotal story, it survives. The sagas, the sacred stories, and the myths are not lies. These are linguistic tools we have invented to help us reach beyond the visible to experience realities that impact us beyond the everyday warning of the real lion about eating the unfortunate gazelle.

Someone in a *sapiens* clan *imagined* a large and successful hunt. They then communicated the vision both within and beyond a single clan. If adequate cooperation ensued, the imagined possibility of a successful large hunt happened. Thus, an essential outgrowth of language was the ability of *sapiens* to secure cooperation for an *imagined* hunt or celebration or deity beyond their eyes. They created that vaunted symbolic world. In time, shamans told the stories of great hunts made possible, they would suggest by spirits, forces, or wonder of wonder gods. In our language, they mythologized those courageous hunts from their dim and distant past.

History suggests the larger the community that is emotionally sustained by the mandated story, the harder to maintain the group's solidarity around the non-visible. Often, when the myth fragments, leaders whose best interests lie in keeping the myth alive, resort to other, often harsh means to enforce the story. Powerful cadres of priests and ecclesiastical hierarchies assure resistors that a terrible fate awaits them in and beyond this life if they do not adhere to the myth. Deprivation, torture, fiery, everlasting hell, slow but eternally smoldering garbage dump, Gehenna, outer darkness, and gloom and doom await questioners, the *fringers* of the sacred story.

Our United States of America is built on the Declaration of Independence, our founding myth. The myth intones that everyone in the community is, by birthright, equal and endowed by *The Creator* no one has ever seen, with certain unalienable rights only recently envisioned. The invisible nation creates laws and social and military institutions that can unevenly maintain the myth. A myth, like any human invention, can become outmoded. When that happens, someone has to burnish the saga, create a new one out of the old, or birth an entirely new, sustaining story. Those with power invested in the story can enforce allegiance to the failing myth by cultural, legal, economic and/or military means. Thus, *Homo sapiens'* ability with language is both a blessing and a curse. Like any human craft, it has the capacity to benefit the adherents or dehumanize the marginalized on the edges of the organization. Throughout the Homo sapiens' years, we have had great and noble as well as mean and terrible examples of the use and abuse of language.

Beware of any generation that seems lost without a leader.
That search may become a dangerous thing to do.
A society that is fearful, money-worried
Anxious for order, hungry for law
A nation of wall builders, accustomed to war
Watching enemies within an enemy without
Afraid it's glory will fade:
Longing for the strong man grows ever so quietly

While people look the other way.

Help us, O Spirit
Not to flirt with forces so ancient and so evil
Rather let us put our trust in you
That justice never bends to fear
Nor freedom to false gods of power.[11]
—Steven Charleston

How Our Great-Grandparents of 20,000 BCE Lived

To understand our *Homo sapiens* ancestors in the wake of the cognitive revolution, from 30,000 to 12,000 BCE, and the dawning of the agricultural revolution, we must get an idea of what their lives were like in those seminally formative millennia.

Until the era of the agricultural revolution, the five to eight million *Homo sapiens* on the Earth lived as hunters and gatherers. As Homo sapiens scattered from Africa beginning in about 100,000 BCE, the environments in which they settled played a determinative role in the way they functioned and thrived. Evolution inexorably shaped and in turn was shaped by the culture. Early *sapiens* typically lived in singular, small groups. Even groups living in close proximity to each other would have different languages, rites, rituals, and diets, hence diverse cultures. Surely, from time to time, the clans would cooperate in gathering and hunting food, but there is little evidence of genuine cooperation and understanding from one small clan to another.

Today's evolutionary psychologists maintain that many of our current habits, proclivities, diet, sexuality, and worldview were shaped by *sapiens* in those millennia leading up to the agricultural revolution. They say we still live unconsciously in the world of hunters and gatherers. Our twenty-first century DNA was encoded millennia ago. Conflict and confusion arising in our lives and institutions in the last few thousand years and, particularly in what we call the modern age, bubble and boil as our collective human psyche tries to reconcile our hunter/gatherer DNA with the way we live now.

Society renames and redefines the objects of our hunting and gathering. By and large we do not have to forage for daily food. Our hunting and gathering ancestors, in their good times at least, had a more nutritious organic diet than we do. We surely do scramble every day to gather enough money to pay for what we think we must hunt and gather. Who needs a closet full of shirts, pants, dresses, shoes, etc.? We do not need superyachts costing $300 million. Our ancestors knew they were hunting and gathering food. Today we spend millions of dollars trying to decide what we want to hunt and gather.

None of us seriously want to go back to those days when today's meal depended on our success at hunting and gathering that day. Still, it could be most helpful in today's scramble to understand better what makes us tick and where the tick comes from. Where does the tick come from to gorge on greasy food and sweets? Our hunter-gatherer ancestors had little access to sweet foods. Sweets came primarily from ripe fruit. When a *sapiens* clan came upon a fig bush full of ripe fruit, they gorged themselves eating all they could before the bonobos found the bush. The propensity to stuff ourselves with sweet and unhealthy food comes from the hardwire of our DNA bequeathed to us by our sweet-hungry *sapiens* ancestors.

Not all *sapiens* lived in small clans. A cadre of evolutionary psychologists suggests that other groups of *sapiens* did not live in monogamous nuclear families but in communes. A female could have sex with as many male members of the commune as she chose and/or who would indulge her. These free-love communes opined she needed to have sex with several men during pregnancy because their intercourse/spirit would make for a better, more well-rounded baby. The verve from smart, strapping, happy, social, expert hunter males could be passed on to the baby. The communes likewise took joint responsibility for child rearing since no one could be sure who the father was.

Perhaps many in our modern society who go through frequent divorces have inherited a super-dose of DNA from *sapiens* communes in which monogamy did not prevail. The monogamous nuclear family may still be the accepted norm but we must not overlook the divorce rate in much of the world. Remember also that more women today are deciding to select the male sperm of their choice for impregnation. After the moment, the man goes his way perhaps to offer his wares to another woman while the single mother purposefully raises the child on her own. DNA has a way of surfacing as it will.

The bottom line of all these theories points to the fact that our *sapiens* ancestors lived and clustered in a wide variety of ways. In the twenty-first century, their multiple-choice genes find abundant lodging.

Ever since the cognitive revolution, no single norm or settled configuration for our *Homo sapiens* ancestors has prevailed. The collateral consequence of the development of language has fostered human diversity from the get-go. Environment shapes language and then language finds ways to accommodate and shape the environment. Iterations of English are the norm for language in the United States.

We have clusters of people, such as Cajuns in the Louisiana coastal regions, who largely speak a different language from the rest of us when they are talking with each other. Most communities in the United States have seen a steady influx of people who speak Spanish or variations of Spanish. It is now fully acceptable in most parts of the country that public signs are presented in Spanish and English. Trams zipping airline passengers from one terminal to the next post all of their directions and destinations in multiple languages. The point is, language is important in building community, and at the same time, dividing us into different communities. The biblical story of the Tower of Babel points to the problem of multiple languages that our Hebrew ancestors understood as they lived in diverse communities 3,000 years ago.

In the millennia leading up to the agricultural revolution, some animals were domesticated. The dog is certainly the first of these and by far the most ubiquitous. Archeologists can confidently trace domesticated dogs to about 35,000 years ago. Other studies push this back even further to 50,000 BCE. Wolves gave us dogs. At some point a pack of wolves evidently produced a mutation breed that became adaptable to human contact. From their earliest existence, dogs were used for companionship, hunting, and as an alarm warning of danger and strangers. Dogs that showed a propensity for companionship got extra care and food. This sense of companionship between master and dog moved ahead on evolution's inevitable if slow-moving tide, becoming etched in the psyche of humans and canines.

Trade, if it could be called such, was confined to a few scarce items such as shells, rocks, or pigments of special significance. Clans were not dependent on one another for food. Other than occasional large hunts, they did their own foraging. Some may have moved with the seasonal migration of animals but invariably returned to what they regarded as their home territory.

Sapiens foraged for more than food. They needed knowledge of the outer reaches of their own tiny territory; where were canyons for trapping game, what plants were growing and where? They sought the lairs of predators and manageable waterways. Where could they find deposits of stones for axes, flint knives, and spear points. This intelligence foraging enhanced the carefully honed skills of *Homo sapiens* ancestors. The clan's experts in flint chipping could make an arrowhead in a few minutes because he had received training handed down for decades. Foraged information could also spark clan by clan trickles of migration to other, more hospitable locations.

Living in those far-flung places with only the resources of one's clan forced *sapiens* to acquire a wide array of skills and sensitivities. They had to understand the weather, winds, and sounds. Rustling in the grass could indicate a venomous snake. Leaves dancing in the wind could alert one to a thunderstorm brewing or ripe fruit within the bowers of the tree. *Sapiens* developed the stamina of marathon runners. They were also susceptible to illness and injury often sending them to early graves. Anthropology has likewise indicated that some lucky humans could live to the advanced age of sixty years and more. All in all, the *sapiens* foragers were more knowledgeable about their own world than anyone else in history. Today we collectively have far more knowledge than our ancestors. We, however, know and understand little beyond our own, often highly technical niche. Survival for *sapiens* demanded a broad understanding of their world and their own bodies, exceeding our highly compartmentalized learning.

Wanderlust Hits *Sapiens*

Until the beginning of the agricultural revolution, *Homo sapiens* lived almost exclusively in the Afro-Asian portion of the earth. Plants, humans, and animals in areas beyond the Afro-Asian landmass developed along their own evolutionary lines. The oceans between these scattered outposts made travel from Afro-Asia impossible. *Homo sapiens* were about to change all of this.

Millennia before the agricultural revolution, *sapiens* had steadily begun to develop both vision and technology to break out of the landlocked area in which they had lived for hundreds of thousands of years. The first target of this breakout was Australia some 45,000 years ago.

Adventurous *sapiens* living on islands part of the Indonesian archipelago developed the technology to build seafaring boats, forming the first mini-maritime culture. The crossings from island to island were still quite formidable because many sea channels, some more than 60 miles wide, had to be navigated. The sea journey from Afro-Asian territory is one of the most significant journeys in history. For the first time people crossed a large body of water.

When *sapiens* stepped onto the Australian beaches, they entered a gigantic landmass that had never seen a human in its eons of existence. *Sapiens* became the first humans of any species to get to the down-under continent of Australia. As the first humans on that continent, *sapiens* had to adjust quickly to a completely different ecosystem. The Australia ecosystem likewise had to learn about these strange creatures moving about on two spindly legs.

Those sea-faring *sapiens* may have understood themselves to be adventurers. In reaching Australia, they were in fact, conquerors. They did not simply adjust to the new ecosystem; they completely transformed their new habitat. Within a few millennia, *sapiens* had moved to the top of the food chain. To achieve this milestone *Homo sapiens* had become deadly predators. Huge marsupials inhabited Australia where they had roamed freely for hundreds of thousands of years. Two-ton diodones, 450-pound kangaroos, marsupial lions as large as tigers, wolf-size rodents, flightless birds twice the size of ostriches sprinted across the plains and hills. Distressingly, these free ranging creatures steadily and dreadfully fell prey to hungry, skilled, and lethal *sapiens*.

These humans had come to Australia with steadily developing hunting skills and equipment. They multiplied rapidly, requiring more and more food. *Sapiens* long ago had mastered fire which gave them the fierce ability to burn large areas of the feeding grounds of all fauna but especially for large marsupials. Thus, within a few millennia, all these giant Australian animals had become extinct. The same relentless predation accompanied *sapiens* wherever they moved. Giant mammoths, mastodons, huge lions, elephants in time fell to the food and hide demands of our *sapiens* ancestors.

Sapiens were smarter, could communicate, would cooperate with others when it suited them, made more deadly weapons for hunting (and conquest), had more babies, and were hungrier. Wherever *sapiens* roamed, large animals provided food, pelts for clothing, and bones both for tools and for sculpting objects of art. They did not count the cost of their voracious appetites sated by the butchering of animals. Besides, for millennia, the hills, forests, and verdant plains seemed to offer an endless supply of food and fur.

Invariably the Walmart-style availability of animals disappeared in specific region, wiped out and consumed much faster than the animals could reproduce. Migration to a new place became the most promising solution to the new normal of scarcity. So *sapiens* continued to spread not only in Australia but everywhere. Resilient *sapiens* simply rose to the challenge of new habitats and fresh supplies of prey. So, our ancestors stayed on the move. Not in mass migration but in inexorable drips and drabs.

Sapiens were the first humans to reach the western hemisphere land mass 16,000 years ago. They walked, carrying their few belongings on their backs. At that time water levels were low enough so that a land bridge connected northeastern Siberia with northwestern Alaska. It was an arduous trek. Humans had to survive the bitter cold climates of Siberia and Alaska. Restless *sapiens* learned to cope with the frigid climate by making snowshoes, and thanks to the needle, could sew together multi-layered clothing. Over the centuries, these intrepid humans kept pushing, opening new frontiers for themselves. They made it into North America and ultimately to the tip of South America.

History had never witnessed such a rapid spread of humans until *sapiens* marched resolutely throughout much of the world. The speed and success of *sapiens* migration in North and South America testifies to the species' aggression, ingenuity, creativity, and resilience. By the beginning of the agricultural revolution in 12,000 BCE, *sapiens* had left a 2,000-year-old trail of blood and rampage. *Sapiens* outthought, out-hunted, and out-birthed animals and plants that had flourished unhindered in the Americas for hundreds of thousands of years. By 13,000 BCE, all was gone.[12]

In Harmony with Nature?

That our ancestors lived in harmony with nature is a myth that modern earth science has put to shame. We have not lived in harmony with nature. We have invariably devastated nature in the name of progress.[13]

The decimation of nature picked up intensity with the agricultural revolution. Until the industrial revolution, the creatures of the sea had existed in relative safety. Then with advancing technology, fueled by greed and overuse, whales, sharks, tuna, and many other species are in danger of being wiped out as sapiens inflict lethal damage. Only we *sapiens* can restore balance between us and nature's order.

Earth scientists have painfully declared, after decades of careful study, that *Homo sapiens* mass migration into the Americas, Europe, Australia and Afro-Asian regions is the largest ecological disaster in 2.5 million years of human history.[14] In the last three millennia, *sapiens* has inhabited remote islands that hitherto had no human presence. The minute *sapiens* steps on the beaches, devastation of animals and plants begins unabated.

Internalize Harari's somber declaration: "The agricultural revolution is history's biggest fraud."[15] I will leave that startling, counter-cultural story to someone else.

Now What?

The obvious, critical question of the age is, what do we *Homo sapiens* do? How do we make the most of our big brains, ingenuity, technological skills and resilience to preserve the planet that we alone have populated for 12,000 years?

As a *Homo sapiens* person, confessionally, I come late to my level of understanding of our often scorched-earth history. Now, as never before, I am alerted, fearful, and with all our ability, hopeful, that we will decide to take an existential oath to honor and respect our planet. Earth, as far as anyone knows, is the nursery, uniquely blessed in all the vast universe, to care for the splendid home which we share with seven billion of our fellow human beings.

I choose to stop here in my personal exploration as a *Homo sapiens* person. These months of fascinating study have opened my mind and spirit to the wonders, awe and, yes, wariness of our individual and collective ability to reaffirm the gorgeous doxology in Genesis: God looked at the world and said, "That's good!"

I believe you and I are more than water
Chemicals and electricity
We are more than winners of a cosmic lottery
That grants life and consciousness at random
And only for a few brief years.

I believe in the soul,
That strange and wonderful mystery of the human spirit
The inner vibration we feel that resonates with our mind
A source of life that is older than the stars
We are beings of a deep awareness
Living memories of a time before time.[16]
 —Steven Charleston

Notes

[1] Tonelli, Genesis.
[2] Charleston, Spirit Wheel, 108.
[3] Tonelli, Genesis.
[4] Harari, Sapiens, i-ii.
[5] Ibid, 9.
[6] Ibid, 8.
[7] Ibid, 19.
[8] Ibid, 20.
[9] Ibid, 23.
[10] Ibid, 23.
[11] Charleston, Spirit Wheel, 203.
[12] Harari, Sapiens, 72.
[13] Ibid, 71.
[14] Ibid, 78.
[15] Ibid, 79.
[16] Charleston, Spirit Wheel, 42.

I Am a Secure Affirming Life-force Person

Imagination must have a greater role in all aspects of the religious life. When imagination fails doctrines become ossified, witness and proclamation wooden, doxologies empty consolations hollow and ethics legalistic.[1]

I intuit that the beginning universe, our planet, and collective humanity throbs, pulsates with before-Genesis generative Life-force. With John Shelby Spong, in his multiple writings, I joyfully experience the on-my-side Life-force as love. Wisely and happily, I locate my existence within the "day without a yesterday" Life-force.

This Life-force Is Beginning

It is not productive to define the Life-force. We can experience the Life-force. How then does one experience the Life-force? Bishop Spong says it beautifully and comprehensively: "Live fully, love extravagantly and be all that I can be."[2]

The Yes, No, and Not so Fast of Language

In talking about YHWH, God, Adonai, the Holy, we need to acknowledge the approximation hermeneutic.

At best, language is our human attempt to embrace the intangible, the impenetrable, the boundary-less of our immediate senses. In that vein, it helps me to understand that language is always a guess at what might be real, approximation, metaphor, aphorism, poetry, and/or imagination.

As I proceed to talk about the Jewish/Christian God by declaring there is *no The Creator*, I am forced to use words and language. That's the only tool at my disposal. Using theological and philosophical words, I hasten to remind myself (and I hope you) that we are immediately in the realm of approximation and imagination when we talk religion of whatever stripe. Put aside absolutes. Shelve church talk. Realize that the men and a few women who gave us God and the Bible, humans like us, were bound by the same restrictions and liberties imposed by the approximations of language even at its very best.

Consider the language of the Hebrew Bible. The ancient Israelites were among the earliest cultures to formulate an alphabet, that is the adaptation of a set of symbols to catch sounds. They then, over time, began to connect the symbols to create words, that is symbols of thought and nature. For centuries, writing and reading belonged to the elites, especially priests who guarded their linguistic skills as trade secrets; not so the sixth century BCE Israelite scribes. These gifted artists of language wrote in vernacular Hebrew, an astounding gift to Israelite street-people of 2500 BCE. Even then, it was fairly early into the use of their developing Hebrew language (that's a fascinating study for PhD linguistic scholars).

Remember, also, that in the grand sweep of evolution, language, preserved history, is a recent human invention. If life forms have been evolving for something like two billion years, human language (sound making goes way back) is only a few hundred thousand years old. We *Homo sapiens* brought campfire language to new levels of skill maybe 100,000 years ago so we do well to keep the novelty of human speech in perspective.

With the approximation hermeneutic as a filter, I venture to declare *no The Creator* and I readily join that great cloud of *fringers* trying to find footing on and for my own shaky ground of being.

Language can get tired. Every day, thousands of church people stand and repeat by memory the Nicene Creed. Thousands more repeat the Lord's Prayer. The Nicene Creed additionally is the orthodox statement of the essence of Christianity. We surely do need to look more closely at that statement hammered out by a group of fourth century clerics who had, according to tradition, been ordered by the

Emperor Constantine to quit their squabbling and decide on the meaning of Christianity. Under pressure, these men cobbled together the Creed. That was 1,500 years ago. Nothing in heaven and earth is the same anymore. The language and theology of the Nicene Creed are beyond credibility, yet the Creed holds.

Not only the creeds, so much of our religious language is in critical need of large doses of hard-headed and open-minded scrutiny. Potentially rich concepts like incarnation, original sin, atonement theology, scripture, resurrection, eschatology, and miracles have lost their punch and their relativity in a culture inundated by a daily fare of new stuff. The words of the preacher, prayers and hymns echo with little resonance among church people. The concepts have value, but the language has lost imagination, creativity, and inwardness thus conveying little meaning.

We are keepers of many mysteries:
How the human heart endures, why love never grows old,
Where to find the wild places when you need them.
We learned all this together. How could I forget?

We carry the same message into the world:
Hope when hope seems fragile
Courage when courage is needed
Faith in what we cannot see until we do.[3]
   —Steven Charleston

Human Words Created the Creator

I indicated in my opening comments that I award history's all-time first prize for poetry and imagination to the classic origins story in the Hebrew Bible's Book of Genesis. Countless generations of us humans around the world have told and retold this classic creation saga. I honor the Hebrew scribes from 2,500 years ago. They crafted their imaginative campfire chants into the soaring flights of enduring metaphorical language that have shaped our theology and even everyday cosmology down to this day.

The sixth century BCE Hebrew scribes intended to offer generative hope to the Israelite remnant after their devastating conquests wrought by two mighty imperial armies. The anonymous scribes brought order out of chaos, rhapsodized a world shaped by care, humanity, love and goodness and gave us the soaring poetry of Genesis 1 and 2.

The Genesis myth honors work in contrast to extravagant privilege. Male and female share equally the "divine" DNA. Humans are stewards not liege lords of all we survey.[4]

My reverence for these narratives notwithstanding, in the twenty-first century, I say there is *no The Creator* of the universe. The universe is yet becoming and unfolding by the force of its own unbounded energy.

In an interview about black holes, Albert Einstein opened up about his personal religious perspective: "The knowledge of something we cannot penetrate, a manifestation of the profoundest reason, a thing of radiant beauty, it is this knowledge, this emotion that constitutes the truly religious attitude. It is in this sense that I am a truly religious man.[5]

Okay, *no The Creator*. That translates for me to no daily heavenly companion. I do existentially sense an impenetrable, friendly mystery, an acknowledged unknowable, a gift from the universe to us, the Spirit by whatever name you give her. Stay with me.

For multiple millennia, women and men like those in the Matthew 2:1-2 birth story of Jesus, have invested their lives in gazing at the night sky, trying to puzzle out what they could and could not see. In our era, gigantic telescopes and billion-dollar space probes roam the universe searching for more clues. Smart women and men who make and manage these machines have resolved numerous vexing questions. For instance, the charged particles of the universe "on a day with no yesterday" squeezed together, then exploded into the Big Bang 13.5 billion years ago. The Earth indeed revolves around the sun and dependably turns on its own axis. We creatures of Earth, at the level of daily existence, count on the stability of sunrise and sunset. In the same breath, we acknowledge that we do live in a wandering universe on a wandering star.

While affirming something as stupendous as the Big Bang, the brightest astronomical minds among us humbly admit we have just begun to pry answers from the secretive universe. Brashly touted final, definitive statements only invite challenge, revision, or abandonment. Still, we try. So cautiously and humbly at 88 years of age, I say, there is *no The Creator* of the universe.

Lest hubris eclipse humility, what I do not know is every bit as large as the Milky Way. Hear me say then, *pigs may yet fly*. Probably not anytime soon and most likely never. Yet, it would be the height of arrogance on my part to say that pigs will *never* fly. So, with today's pigs penned up on the Earth and not winging in the sky, l say there is *no The Creator*.

Lay Aside Questions of Theodicy

To say there is *no The Creator* is to put to rest the other ageless question: how can a good and just God allow so much evil in the world? Answer: there is no *Creator* God, good or evil, so there is no theodicy issue. Evil exists in the world because we continue to produce people who choose to be and do evil.

The world was jarred awake September 9, 2023, with breaking news that a cataclysmic earthquake had leveled vast sections of Morocco. On the heels of the quake, floods in Libya killed more than 5,000 people. Lethal tornadoes, hurricanes, floods, raging forest fires, plagues and famine happen as part of the natural order of the universe. These disasters, albeit unpredictable, can be scientifically explained. All too often the loss of life in these catastrophes can be laid at the feet of our collective greed-driven actions or inactions.

God had nothing to do with the Holocaust because there is no God to allow or stop such horrors. Unspeakably evil men and women caused the Holocaust. Unspeakably evil women and men have created and perpetuated antisemitism, anti-black, anti-gay, anti-Asian, anti-Irish, anti-Italian, you name it, we collectively have done it. We are Lucy who invariably moves Charlie Brown's football.

I have stood on the edge of a midnight canyon
And called out the question into silent shadows: Why?

But suffering will not have the last word
Not without challenge.

We may not know the reason
But we will have the dignity of the question.[6]
—Steven Charleston

Where are we then? *Homo sapiens* are the only remaining human species on the planet. That means we, not God, are responsible to change attitudes, hearts, politics, environment, and daily deeds. Those critical changes must begin in and emanate from my spirit and yours.

So, the Myth

Both the Hebrew Bible and the Christian Testament contain a few generative myths and a host of grand, rich stories. To my way of thinking, the Hebrew Bible offers two preeminent myths: creation in Genesis 1 and 2 and the saga of the Hebrews' exodus from Egypt. The early Jesus movement launched on the resurrection of Jesus.

Both parts of the Bible offer a wealth of masterful stories full of drama and wisdom: Abraham, Joseph, David and Goliath, etc. In the Christian Testament, these include stories of Jesus' birth, walking on water, feeding the five thousand, Paul's Damascus Road experience, etc.

The creating God of Genesis is a splendid myth. Myth is good. Myth is a story, saga, drama or epic poetry that wraps itself around a cherished hope or tradition. A myth wants to sing to the heart what mind and reason cannot affirm.

For millennia, humans and especially, for the last 100,000 years, many of our species have generated heavenly gods to thank when good stuff happens. We have created scapegoats to blame for all the bad stuff that happens to good people. We have pined for and sung about a heavenly friend who can give us a happily-ever-after especially if we pray fervently enough or make sacrifices to him/her/them.

Our Hebrew ancestors, in trying to explain the potential demise of their ways of life and in a myriad of different iterations, created, evolved, and celebrated the God, YHWH, of the Bible and culture. We blissfully perpetuate the comforting and challenging myth while contending with a multitude of theistic contradictions.

For a myth to serve its purpose, we need to get inside the myth. What is the poet-author of the myth trying to convey? What is her purpose in taking pen to paper and transcribing her story?

Let's offer a tip of the hat to biblical scholar John Dominic Crossan: "My point once again is not that those ancient people told literal stories and we are now smart enough to take them symbolically, but they told them symbolically and we are still dumb enough to take them literally."[7]

As myths go, our Jewish/Christian take on YHWH of the Hebrew/Christian Bible is quite new, maybe 3,000-2,500 years old. In the grand million-year sweep of human existence, factoring in *Homo* genus maybe 800,000 years ago and *sapiens* 300,000 years ago, our Hebrew/Christian Adonai/God is but a blip among many blips.

The Hebrew's YHWH is a synthesis of ca 5,000 BCE theisms from the Middle East. Our Hebrew ancestors became persuaded that the many gods of the diverse tiny kingdoms among which they lived were inadequate and morally unworthy. Curating the campfire stories of the host of gods they had to keep happy, our Hebrew ancestors took courage and gradually generated the idea of one YHWH. That made more sense and helped make religious life more manageable. The sixth century BCE Hebrew scribes draped a sensible, covenantal theology around their one and only YHWH above the several YHWHs of their neighboring Near Eastern kingdoms.

The allegiance to the one God took a long time to take hold, though actually never completely. Some of the psalms declare that YHWH is superior to other gods thus admitting the presence of competing deities.

Neighbors among whom the Israelites lived (ca tenth to sixth centuries BCE) had robust festivals and carnal pleasures in the celebrations of their hilltop gods. Fun-hungry Israelites looked with longing eyes on their neighbors' gatherings in the name of religion while garnering scorn and doom from their Hebrew prophets.

Finally, after hundreds of years of theological and cultural hassle, the majority of by then Jews, more or less agreed on the one God, YHWH. Over the course of time, they passed their monotheism on to the aborning Jesus movement. We should note that our Jewish and Christian ancestors did not lack spectacles and festivals while apparently eschewing sexual bacchanals.

Why Not the Best?

It needs to be said quickly that the one YHWH the Israelites generally came to worship called for the best from themselves and the rest of humanity. Through the honorable prophets, their YHWH communicated equal love for all of humanity and the universe he had spoken into existence. He also spoke justice into the world with a clear voice: "Let justice roll down like water." (Amos 5:24); "Love your neighbor as yourself." (Leviticus 19:18)

The Babylonian world into which the elite of conquered Judah was thrust had its own creation myths. They were full of dragons, huge snakes, blood, and wild sex. The Israelite scribes of the sixth century BCE rejected those tumultuous Babylonian myths. The Israelite scribes gave their distressed Israelite expatriates the Genesis story of a loving Elohim/YHWH speaking the world into existence. That Genesis myth has stayed with us Westerners. Along the way, we morphed that poetic myth into quasi science, the orthodox word on creation, to which all God-fearing people adhered. I celebrate the Genesis story—just make sure it is poetry and imagination. Hold it lovingly with one side of your brain while opening the other side for something like The Big Bang.

God and Culture

I grew up in the 1950s Baptist south among people and preachers talking about God. This God they typically described was good as long as I was good. He, always male, was on my side if I stayed on his side. When I grew older and broadened my religious experience beyond the Baptist south, I encountered people who talked and preached about this God as one who loves and cares for me and the rest of us *sapiens* regardless of our bad habits. Our Baptist preachers told us that God regularly intervenes in the daily stuff of our lives particularly if we pray earnestly for his help. More theologically generous people also said God feels the pain of the death and destruction of humanity when bad things happen. He feels the pain that he either caused or allowed to happen? He stood on the sidelines wringing his hands and weeping while six million of our fellow human beings were murdered? That's hard theology for me to swallow.

As I mentioned earlier, we must constantly defend this God because his alleged direct and indirect actions in the world are so often monumentally indefensible. We collectively and individually have had no good, reasonable answer to that thorny question: why evil? In trying to explain something as horrible as the Holocaust, World War II, or genocide in Rwanda we spend enormous mental energy burying our heads in the sand (a few salty friends describe another place where we bury our heads) while trying to defend God.

A few centuries ago, Satan began to appear in religious literature. Where did Satan come from? Did God, as ruler of the universe, create a malevolent Satan? Did God throw up his hands in despair over the mess we humans were making of his grand creation so that he decided to set the devil loose in the world? us? How can a good God allow so much evil?

Historically, through a long, completely human process Jews and Christians invented Satan in a lame attempt to keep God's righteous skirts clean. The invention of Satan does not let the hoped-for all good and loving God off the hook.[8]

Does a rose by any other name smell the same? We must go beyond conjuring up a new smell for the God myth. A nod of the head, a shrug of the shoulders does not short-circuit the encounter with the electric, cosmic *energy* that showered the void with stardust, a Life-force impregnated with everything necessary for at least thirteen billion years for the universe and our becoming. Our dynamic universe looks askance at gods, good or evil. We are it!

Life-force, First and Last

I am not made in the image of God because there is no God to cast the image. If *no the Creator*, I affirm a life-giving, love-energizing, Stardust-imbued, on-my-side impenetrable, beckoning, non-gender, non-being Life Force. With radical humility, I affirm I

If *no the Creator*, I affirm a life-giving, love-energizing, Stardust-imbued, on-my-side impenetrable, beckoning, non-gender, non-being Life Force.

am cast in the image of our collective humanity stretching back a million years. I am cast in the image of Bob Maddox, Sr., Dorothy Cook, Miss Ethel Jones, Bill Lawson, George Cowden, Bill Rogers, Dan McGee, and Jesus to name only a few standouts. I'm also made in the image of bad people. The Hebrew scribes distilled from their complex picture of sixth century BCE YHWH the dimensions of care for each other and stewardship of our home earth. With these images embedded, *I want to love extravagantly, be all that I can be, and live fully.*[9]

Here's what beckons me like the dawning of a new day:

I would not sacrifice my soul
for all the beauty of this world.

There is only one thing
for which I would risk everything:
an I-don't-know-what
that lies hidden
in the heart of the Mystery.[10]
  —John of the Cross

My dear friend and mentor Dr. Dan McGee gets breathtakingly inside the life-restoring story with:

"The Invitation of the Unknowable"

The Unknowable:
We are blest with the quest
Of the Unknowable,

And twice blest by Resting within it.
Within the heart of mystery
Lies that which
The human mind need not fathom
Fully to embrace life's transcendent gifts.

From roiling times
Emerges that which pales
The fear of the unknown.

The quest for the Unknowable,
Ah, that's life's reason for being
and final place of rest. [11]

Note: These adventure-filled decades of discovery and liberation have gifted me with the spiritual and academic courage to take this enchanting *no The Creator* "road less traveled."

As a *no The Creator* person in the twenty-first century, I can let the universe be the universe. I read (often listen with Audible) in amazement Copernicus, Galileo, Newton, Einstein, Hawking, Tonelli, Harari, and more. I meet science again for the first time synthesized by the likes of Joy Hakim in her inviting three-volume *Story of Science*. I come away from these eye-opening works with the strong conviction that the universe, Earth and we are self-generating, literally impregnated by the gift of star dust from at least 13.5 billion years ago.

We can play the "gotcha" game by teasing: who or what caused the Big Bang? God or somebody must be behind that cosmic phenomenon, we opine. Nope, not God. Not anybody. In a self-generated moment, all the particles of the void coalesced, then inevitably overburdened, overcooked by that much cosmic matter in one place, in a second to a million minuses unburdened itself and exploded. Since energy is neither created nor lost, latent energy collected itself. Then losing nothing, energy redistributed that vast nuclear, radioactive pile into the void. The Big Bang keeps banging. It is still doing its thing in the expanding universe, irrevocably evolving in fruit flies, sperm whales and in you and me.

Thank you, ancient Hebrew BCE scribes, from war-torn, laid-waste Israel and Judah with twentieth century poets like James Weldon Johnson (*God's Trombones*) for opening your faithing and soaring spirits to us giving soul-enriching stories. In the twenty-first century let their stories be just that: life-enriching stories. Do not burden early Genesis with cheap, struggling, embarrassing, even corny science. The Hebrew poets did not know about the Big Bang and James Weldon Johnson sang beyond it.

Big Bang as Macro

The Genesis God as *Creator* is long overdue for a happy, peaceful retirement. Maybe it is that the universe runs on its own steam or more accurately nuclear energy. No *Creator*. No heavenly mechanic. No divine conductor. The universe stays at its *macro* task of beginning because of the Big Bang.

Sapiens as Micro

The fundamental, intuited mystery, spirit, or collective energy of unnumbered *Homo sapiens* performs the microtasks of connecting us to each other, of curing Alzheimer's disease, of rebuilding fractured families and communities. It is ours to do with skill and compassion, the never-ending microwork vouch-faced to us by the self-generating universe.

Maybe *we* are collectively the mystery, the spirit born from the subatomic particle to the oft-ragged, sometimes magisterial march of genus *Homo sapiens*, the impenetrable, since Georges Lemaitre's "day with no yesterday."

A New Way: Possibilianism

A generative path, still unfolding, may pull my basics together: *possibianism*, an approach to life flagged by Dr. David Eagleman in his book *Incognito*, lectures and media appearances. Why not revel in the alternatives; why not imagine us as bits of networked hardware in a cosmic program, or as particles (*stardust*) of some celestial organism, or any one of a thousand other possibilities, then test those ideas against the evidence. Part of the scientific temperament is tolerance for holding multiple hypotheses at a single time. As Voltaire said, "Uncertainty is an uncomfortable position, but certainty is an absurd one." Given the incredible leaps we humans have made collectively, with all we *sapiens* have accomplished, considering what we know and what we know we do not know, I cautiously hold open the possibility that *pigs may yet fly*.[12]

Dr. Bill Rogers on Possibilianism:

My stories are to be taken symbolically.
Free from doctrine; full of awe.
I am in awe of unconditional love.
I am in awe of the inherent dignity, and worth of all beings.
I am in awe of this pale blue dot hurtling through the cosmos.

I am a Possibilian
The possibilian believes we know one thing: what we don't know and that will change.[13]

Dr. Ed Schrader,[14] scientist and educator, in his own unfolding credo offers me yet another, intriguing possibilian. Isaac Newton told the world that energy in a closed system is neither created nor destroyed—it only changes form. That law of physics still holds. Energy doesn't vanish; it transforms.

Dr. Schrader reminds humans we are cosmic energy and matter. This gifted scientist ignites me then with a query: what happens to us when we die? Dr. Schrader and a new friend, Dr. Kieffer Hellmeister helped me ever that the physical energy that is us; that animates our bodies, the Life-force from whence we came, isn't lost. It becomes something else. And while neither *Siri* nor I can say where identity or memory might go, the energy of our existence persists, that we rejoin afresh the Life-force from which we began. If we trust that we are never entirely gone, that we are folded back into the universe that birthed us, death can cease to hold such existential terror. We can say with John Donne, "Death be not proud…" Dying may be complicated depending on the circumstances. Marching into the new morning as transformed but never lost energy resounds like Handel's *Hallelujah Chorus* or Beethoven's *Alle Menchen*, an exhilarating flight into poetry and imagination.

We humans are a zillion particles of energy packaged in flesh and bone. The billions of us to whom the cosmos have granted life change but never go away. The universe then is the guardian of gazillion quanta of life-giving, body-healing, hope-generating, love-infusing energy, an inestimable treasure trove of everlasting gifts from The Big Bang. This concept of boundaryless energy likewise invites a dramatic paradigm shift. If we do not have to agonize about our cosmic "ground of being" beyond death we can more seriously concentrate on making this life the best it can be. The Newton-Schrader-Hillmeister theorem flings open wide doors for me: dying is not erasure, it is returned. *Not dust to dust but energy to energy thou returnest!*

Death: When I return "my borrowed life to the universe," let there be rejoicing. I will have found "my own star where I can warm myself." [15]

We Are It!

Question: With God retired, to whom or what do we turn in crisis, in celebration? We do what we have always done—we pray. And nail it down—everyone prays. When your teenager is wracked with leukemia, when the specter of hunger or foreclosure haunts like the Wicked Witch, you pray.

How does prayer work? We can imagine our prayers beaming up to the heavenly call center. In reality, we do what we have always done, individually or collectively, we answer our own prayers. We are praying that the latest medical cocktail created by a host of women and men in long white coats will attack your boy's leukemia. You are praying for a Happy Meal or a friendly banker. There is no God there, but you are reinforced by a million years of human history.

Foreclosure—as bad as it is—can be managed because you have the spirits of your ancestors and bodies of friends who are huddling nearby to help you over the hump. You answer your *sapiens* neighbor's prayer by "doing unto her as she/they will do unto you." Golden rule or cosmic stuff? Same difference.

While I am talking about prayer, Pete Davis, one of my best friends and undaunted explorer of the challenging has gifted me with a workable Issac Newton take on prayer. If energy is neither created nor lost, when I pray for you, I create an "energy field" between you and me. Beyond my knowing, your prayer/energy field for me can have a positive effect on me, my body, my relationships, etc. Prayer/energy field for Gaza, Ukraine, Trump, Putin, my troubled loved one, or sick friend can make a difference more than previously realized. A mystic long gone talked about prayer as "love energy." As we agree to pray for each other we build community between us. Don't give up on prayer. Refocus your praying. Remember "pigs may yet fly."

News of that devastating and murderous Moroccan earthquake flashed across the news. More than 2,000 Moroccans asleep in their beds would never wake up. Thousands lost in flooded Libya, gone forever. The call for prayers echoed. Remember, we, not the *no The Creator*, answer prayers. What needs to happen in these disasters is millions of us brother and sister *sapiens* should reach deep into our pockets and bank accounts and send tons of money to reputable relief agencies. I tapped into the Red Cross app. Immediately, well-trained, intrepid rescue teams were on their way.

Governments anywhere near a fault line should labor to strengthen homes and buildings doing everything possible to mitigate earthquake damage. A pox on any who say the quake or flood are God's visitation. No god in human imagination had anything to do with the shifting of tectonic plates, part and parcel of this great and terrible wandering star we inhabit. Human inattention to flood protection may well have made the flood worse. But Adonai or Allah had no part in it.

Faithing as Foundation

Comfortable with *no The Creator*, I manage by faithing. My faithing does not locate in an other out there. I do believe in that first atom's energy and order. The universe has its own plan. I do not say "What you see is what you get." The universe and humans are more than the sum of their/our parts, more than meets the eyes of the strongest telescopes or microscopes. Nothing happens in the universe that is beyond its plan. Nothing on Earth is dependable except death.

If mystery exists yet keeps still in the universe, then mystery, spirit, and connectivity work overtime on Earth among us humans. Our indigenous sisters and brothers invoke Spirit to help us locate, to live within the impenetrable.

I am a more-than-meets-the-eye-of-a-telescope-or-microscope person perched, at 88 on the edge of our second great mystery, death having lived fully out of the first great mystery birth with no conclusions and no boundaries.

The human soul is collective rather than singular. We are one and us. We are winners of the cosmic lottery, but more, wondrously more. We are water, chemicals, and electricity, but more. We are made of more than first light and present stardust showering the collected and connected us for 13.5 billion years. We do not calculate the more. We intuit and live the more. And thankfully, that's a start.

Thus, I am a unique yet connected person who has appreciatively retired the Genesis God. I am a more-than-meets-the-eye-of-a-telescope-or-microscope person perched, at 88 on the edge of our second great mystery, death having lived fully out of the first great mystery birth with no conclusions and no boundaries.

Notes

[1] Wilder, *Theopoetic*, 2.

[2] John Shelby Spong, *Unbelievable* (New York, HarperCollins, 2018), 287.

[3] Charleston, *Spirit Wheel*, 124.

[4] Jacob L. Wright, *Why the Bible Began* (United Kingdom, Cambridge University Press, 2023), 160.

[5] Brian Cox and Jeff Forshaw, *Black Holes: The Key to Understanding the Universe* (London, HarperCollins Publishers, 2022), 1.

[6] Charleston, *Spirit Wheel*, 26.

[7] Jon Dominic from lectures, podcasts, media presentations. Dr. Bill Rogers gave this quote to me.

[8] Elaine Pagels, *The Origin of Satan* (New York, Penguin Press, 1995), 56.

[9] Spong, *Unbelievable*, p. 9

[10] From John of the Cross given to me by Dr. Tim Tutt, source unknown.

[11] From Dr. Dan McGee, used with permission.

[12] From Dr. Bill Rogers and Robert Maddox and collected ideas from Dr. David Eagleman.

[13] From Dr. Bill Rogers used with permission

[14] From Robert Maddox in collaboration with Dr. Ed Schrader, a geological scientist and retired university president.

[15] Popova, *The Universe in Verse*, 22.

I Am a "That Something with No Boundaries and No Conclusions Happened 20-to-200 CE" Person

Jesus lived, thought, taught, healed, and died as a Jewish man for whom the God of Genesis and the Hebrew prophets framed his relationship with the Holy. The depth and breadth of that relationship had no bounds. Jesus could have checked the census box: "Yes, I believe in God." Checking the "Yes" box would in no way define or limit his embrace of the Holy.

But—and this a significant pause for me—Jesus was not the only Jew in Judea/Palestine who was a strong, faithful devoted self-giving follower of YHWH/Adonai in 25 CE. Nothing in his résumé would have attracted any significant recognition by those among whom he lived other than his good nature, compassion, wisdom, and some ability as a healer. So why of all the good Galileans did those early devotees of Jesus, especially Paul, settle on Jesus as the unique gift of God to the world?

I do not know. If Jesus died in about 30 CE, no historic notice of him surfaced until Paul wrote the Thessalonian Jesus club a letter in 50 CE. That's a gap of twenty years or so. I hasten to say, in retrospect they were years of ferment for the Jesus people, just largely out of historical sight.

As an interesting sidebar, because of the Great Fire of Rome under Nero in 64 CE, one line of tradition has the emperor blaming followers of Christus for the fire. Another level of history notes that Nero executed 979 Jesus people for starting the firestorm that destroyed much of the teeming city. If that story is true, it is ironic that such early recognition of the Jesus movement came from the venal emperor.

I am intrigued with the massive amount of scholarship that Jon Dominic Crossan has given us in his comprehensive book *The Birth of Christianity*[1] to present strong extrapolated clues that the Jesus movement was serendipitously developing in those decades. I am attempting a novel about those first 30 years that I am calling from *Easter to the Ascension*. Why was that activity bubbling out of plain sight around and for the meaning of the crucified Galilean?

It is obvious that something happened from 20 to 200 CE that draped the very good and caring man with a divinity that has shaped the world for the better part of two millennia.

Ah, you say, we have the gospels that fill in the blanks. But why the gospels? Prevailing scholarship insists that none of the authors ever saw Jesus. Their books are not traditional history. They are faith statements written in heroic genre by devoted second and third generation followers of the post-Easter Jesus, memories of memories with a measure of wishful thinking.

Paul and Mary Magdalene declaim their visions of the risen Jesus that galvanized their devotion to him as God's anointed. Mary's reported visions have perhaps more credibility because gospel accounts recall she spent face-to-face, probably heart-to-heart time with Jesus as a female follower and a person present at the arrest, crucifixion, death, and resurrection of Jesus. The literary world in which Mary and Paul lived and wrote gave significant credibility to visions. Did their ephemeral experiences give us the world-shaping Christian movement? A cluster of *somethings* has given the world the Christian religion.

Disclaimer and Affirmation

Jesus, dying for the sins of all humankind for all time?

For decades I have stumbled over that one. Religion professors in college and seminary tried unsuccessfully for my young, *fringer* mind to give a reasonable explanation to that basic tenet of classic Christology. Yet, as with several other similarly sweeping doctrines, I had nothing in my training at that time to help me stumble through such a theological thicket, so I filed away my questions. Now, at my tender age in 2025, I have shelved that conundrum along with original sin, inerrant Bible, virginal conception, and bodily resurrection

As a Southern Baptist preacher in the over-the-top evangelistic fervor of the post-World War II era, I had a spotty record as a "come to Jesus" revivalist. The number of baptisms the preacher could report every year became a key factor for landing one of those big, prestigious Southern Baptist churches, my goal at the time. Even in those halcyon days of Baptists' domination of southern religiosity, nagging questions about Jesus as savior blunted my evangelistic fervor.

I certainly wanted my congregants to live the "abundant life" (John 10:10). I certainly wanted my churches to grow, to attract more interested people, and to enrich their lives. I could readily build sermons that sought to point toward the Jesus' way of compassion and rich living. I simply could not preach Jesus dying on the brutal cross to get an angry God off my back. My sermons, lacking a bloodied Jesus in a time when Billy Graham was packing in thousands, sounded rather tame, even bland. Search committees of big city Baptist churches rarely hired preachers like me: less-than-stellar "soul winners."

I hasten to say that I loved where I served. Linda and I made lasting friends who thanked us for our ministry. I was quite fulfilled as a pastor and did not want to do anything other than be an effective and caring minister.

I retired the Genesis/Jewish/Christian God, the heavenly father of the Lord Jesus Anointed, who had sent his only son to redeem the world by willingly dying on a cross. With that God in the celestial rocking chair, it follows that I must either abandon or rediscover Jesus.

I choose not to abandon Jesus (I am sure Jesus, wherever he is today, breathes a sigh of relief at my thoughtfulness). I choose to rediscover Jesus for myself in my time.

> **I choose to rediscover Jesus for myself in my time.**

Jesus had a birthday. Born 4 BCE, in the waning days of King Herod the Terrible, he had a mother and a father like every human. Tradition names his parents Mary and Joseph. That works for me. He had brothers and sisters (Mark 6:3). Jesus was probably born and raised in Nazareth, a Galilean village near the large city of Sepphoris, ironically never mentioned in any Christian Testament writings. The Jewish/Greek/Roman city would have dominated the economic and political culture of a considerable swath of Galilee. If Jesus' father was a worker (*tekton*) in wood, as tradition suggests, Sepphoris would have been his major market. With Greek as the *Lingua Franca*, people like Jesus could probably manage both his native Persian/Aramaic and enough street Greek to facilitate connections with the markets and the non-Jews of the city (viz, the millions of bilingual Hispanics and others in the United States). Imperial Rome, with Caesar Augustus as absolute Imperator, ruled the Mediterranean world, Gaul, and much of Britain. Augustus skillfully and brutally created and enforced the *Pax Romana*, primarily by military power. Life for the likes of Mary, Joseph, and Jesus was invariably harsh and often brief.

With understandable caution for fear of retribution, the Christian Testament authors avoided extended criticism of the Empire. Rome, not the noisy Jewish religious parties, was the undeniable enemy. Jesus was executed by the Roman occupying army in collusion with some of the temple power brokers. The "Jews" did not kill Jesus. So, he was born and died—that's the extent of a historically, if sketchy, credible biography for Jesus. Crucifixion was a regular event in much of the Roman Empire, including Judea/Palestine. Jesus' death initially attracted no attention other than from his family and a few of his close followers.

From Jesus to Christianity

The power of Christianity lay not in its promise of other worldly compensation for suffering in this life, as so often been proposed. Know the critical change that took place was the rapidly spreading awareness of a faith that delivered potent antidotes to life's miseries here and now.[2]
—Diana Butler Bass

If Jesus' early 20s CE historicity is thin, twenty-first century Jesus people have substantial help from contemporary biblical scholarship. Thanks to careful scholarly research, linked with a historical discipline, cross-cultural anthropology, reasonable extrapolations can be advanced about Jesus and his time. Today's scholars of the Jesus of history have constructed a *gestalt*, a reasonable profile of a gifted man like Jesus.

Paul's letters (written from about 50 to 60 CE) to aborning Jesus groups scattered in the western reaches of the Roman Empire and the four gospels (the late sixties to early second century CE) give clues about Jesus and the movement that emerged in his name.

The four gospels portray Jesus as a teacher aiming to bring vitality to the ways of the Judaism of his time. He may have employed homespun medical skills consistent with his time. The cures referenced in the gospels focused largely on emotionally induced maladies. For instance, the gospels offer no mention that Jesus healed medical issues such as broken bones.

The gospels reflect the affirmation that Jesus was the unique son of God who could perform miracles of healing and feeding. Persistent bad health and scarce food plagued peasants throughout the Empire, a plight for poor people everywhere in every era. The gospel stories of Jesus having power over these conditions served to strengthen the post-Easter image of Jesus as uniquely gifted by Adonai.

The gospel narratives of Jesus the miracle worker were the products of memory of memories. The four gospels are remarkable faith statements by highly skilled authors written in vernacular (*koine*) Greek to Jesus communities with which they had connections. These documents are written in the laudatory genre making exalted claims that praised noble leaders. In depth study of the gospels is a fascinating pursuit for me that we could talk about later. The gospels do have numerous aspects of mundane history intermingled with loving faith assertions about Jesus.

A small band of devoted men and women, fellow travelers loved and trusted Jesus deeply. They accompanied him in his often-scorned itinerant ministry to small Galilean villages. The villagers typically welcomed his words and ministry while raising the ire of traditionalists.

Jesus vigorously challenged the money-driven temple system, a conflict that may have triggered his death. To add an even heavier weight on Jesus, some of his adoring friends apparently hailed him King of the Jews—a treasonous, capital offense. Rome could have only one ruler, the emperor. Jesus got in even more trouble when some of his followers declared him the (divine) son of God. Again, Rome could have only one divine son and the emperor already had that spot. Between an entrenched Jewish temple hierarchy and the Roman army that tolerated no threat to the empire or ruler, Jesus' days were numbered. Gospel accounts of huge crowds gathering around Jesus is a stretch. The Roman army ruthlessly controlling crowds, simply would not tolerate throngs collecting around a charismatic leader such as Jesus.

The first-century Jesus movement that became the Christian church in the third century CE emerged in the years after his death. Cutting and pasting texts from the Hebrew Bible, Paul and earnest, smart, Greek-speaking early believers decided the crucified Jesus was indeed the long-hinted-at transcendent Son of God.

Paul lived in his religion's centuries of animal sacrifices at the Jerusalem Temple as atonement for sin. In trying to discern the meaning of Jesus 'tragic execution, my theory is Paul decided the death to be a once-for-all all-time sacrificial atonement for sin. Jesus dying on the cross as sacrifice was God's plan to bring about a reconciliation between a righteous God and sinful humanity.

To the contrary, Jesus, as a faithful Jew, would not have identified himself as part of the God design in any special, apocalyptic vein as Paul, the Christian Testament, and orthodox Christian theology has crafted.

Deifying Jesus as God's anointed from before time, a co-creator with God (John 1), was a process of the slow but definite expansion of the adoration of Jesus after he died. For the movement to compete with the elaborate polytheism of the Empire, Jesus had to be more than a good and godly man killed as a threat to entrenched religion and imperial power. Everyone understood people were executed every day for even the smallest threat to Rome's rule. So, the Jesus movement steadily draped Jesus with heavenly honors to strengthen his standing in the Greek and Roman pantheon. Dr. Robert Funk, a noted scholar and founder of the Jesus Seminar, says Paul and other early evangelists had to find a way to "market" Jesus in a highly competitive Greco/Roman religion ethos in the western reaches of the Empire where they concentrated their efforts.[3]

Amos Wilder in *Theopoetics* added to the post-Easter scenario:

When Paul and other missionaries to the gentiles went out into the cities of Asia Minor and Greece, they had to appeal to a different kind of culture. The impulse and meaning of their message depended on a changed rhetoric and appropriate symbols. The terms and categories of their witness had to be modulated to awaken response in a different theater with its own acoustics and its own imaginative repertoire. Their words and their ceremonies carried over into the hearts of people. Because they could reimagine their message they could find a home in the dreams and hungers, the mysteries and mythologies of the Greek world.[4]

Paul and other early missionaries, captivated by their visions of the risen Jesus, were creating their Christology on the road, a work-in-progress as they walked from one Roman city to the next. It is becoming clearer, however, that what the scattered Jesus groups missed in formal Christology they gratefully got his call for compassion, justice, love for everyone, and confrontation with the status quo. For instance, Matthew 25 lifts up the broad ministry of the Jesus group to which he wrote his gospel in the 90s.

Further, I theorize that people in the Galilean villages loved and respected him to such an extent that they were spiritually ready for the exalted preaching from the likes of Paul and perhaps women like Mary Magdalene. These Galilean villagers would not let Jesus "stay" dead, thereby generating or reinforcing the empty tomb Easter story in the four gospels. Writing in 50s CE, Paul hailed the crucified and risen Christ but makes no mention of the Easter stories in the gospels (70 to 120 CE).

Thus, contrary to more conventional suppositions, the Jesus movement did not come roaring full throttle from the cross/resurrection/Pentecost saga. It began in fits and starts with Jesus-people scattered around the Mediterranean world meeting in small house groups. Early evidence indicates they had only a haphazard understanding of Jesus. The question persists—how did these scattered groups happen? Did the early movement produce traveling preachers in addition to the small cadre indicated in the Book of Acts?

The emerging Jesus movement ran on at least two tracks. One is the ongoing debate among early church fathers who boldly declared their pronouncements as the "true" faith, a "Master Story." Current biblical studies ponder these debates. Brandon Scott and Professor Karen King of Harvard challenge the resulting fourth century "Master Story" as flawed orthodoxy.[5] The story proclaims that Jesus came down from heaven and launched Christianity; he performed miracles. Then, before dying, he handed on his complete teachings to his loyal male (no female) followers—the apostles—through apostolic ordination. These, by then, bishops authoritatively passed on the "true" teachings of Jesus. New bishops, likewise, handed on the true faith to men they apostolically ordained. In the fourth century, the same cadre of duly ordained bishops encapsulated the "true" faith in the Nicene and Apostles' Creeds. The "Master Story" stops at the end of the fourth century. Mainline biblical scholars criticize the "Master Story" and ratification of the twenty-seven New Testament documents as inadequate theology and poor history. Enshrining the "Master Story" as the true faith, the bishops stifled imagination for centuries, insisting on old wine in old wineskins. Fortunately, new wine continued to ferment beyond the bishops' scornful eyes.

The second developmental track underscores the day-by-day life of the erstwhile followers of Jesus expanding to various parts of the Empire. Brandon Scott's book *After Jesus* does not labor over the theological debates that swirled in those opening decades. Bishops could argue. The new Jesus people had to feed their families and figure how to live as followers of Jesus under Imperial Rome. In ways still heavily shrouded in history, Jesus house clubs were gathering here and there with disparate ideas about Jesus they collected around what they knew of him. No single grand Pentecost moment as pictured in Acts launched the Christian church. The movement started in drips and drabs led by women and men who displayed vision, courage, and spiritual gifts.[5]

What were those scattered, aborning Jesus groups doing as they tried to put their lives together as people of the Jesus Anointed?

After Jesus Before Christianity gives six hallmarks that characterized first and second century Jesus clubs:[6]

• These gutsy clubs resisted the Roman Empire in multiple subtle counter-imperial ways. For starters, worshipping an Anointed, innocent, good man executed by Rome was a distinct in-your-face to Imperial brutality.

• Life under the Empire's boot prompted gender-bending. Believers lived out Paul's admonition in Galatians, " ... there is no longer slave or free, there is no longer male and female; for all of you are one in Christ Jesus" (Galatians 3:28). Harassed by constant disruptions and violence and exacerbated by relentless economic turmoil, traditional gender roles had to adapt. In some cases, women dressed as men to wend their way through the pervasive social upheavals. With men regularly drafted for forced labor, often sent to distant building projects or enslaved, women exercised leadership roles in unprecedented ways.

• Communities of the Anointed often lived in chosen families. Imperial violence and persistent social dislocations in the Empire forced many in the Jesus groups to adopt creative ways to live together. Torn apart blood-line families were prevented from living together. The Jesus groups coped by reconfiguring family in new ways.

• Since the fifth century BCE, Jews lived throughout the Mediterranean world, making lives for themselves, determined to maintain their Jewishness. Non-Jews who became followers of a Jewish Lord resonated with the ways of their Jewish neighbors. With the Christian Testament 300 years into the future, the Hebrew Bible became the book for numerous Jesus clubs who often identified closely with the God of Jesus and Israel.

• The local Jesus clubs had diverse organizational structures. Ecclesiastical hierarchies did not yet exist or were in flux. The resilient, scattered clubs worked out their own governance and leadership styles, changing steadily as circumstances and social pressures demanded. Naturally, conflicts cropped up as Paul's letters indicate.

Brandon Scott said, "Writing did not dominate the life of the early communities of the Anointed to the same degree as surviving documents have dominated how we have imagined their life."[7] The Anointed groups worshipped based on oral traditions: preaching, teaching, table fellowship, the Eucharist, and baptism.

This outline can whet your appetite to dig more deeply into those first 200 years of the Jesus movement. Certainly, it is a fascinating story of courage, compassion, service, resilience poetry, and imagination. I am grateful to be able to connect with my extraordinary ancestors.

The Jesus groups, increasingly non-Jewish, likewise had only bits and pieces of the Hebrew Greek (Septuagint Bible) to provide any measure of guidance. To be sure, details chronicling the early spread of the Jesus movement are scarce, fostering much stimulating research and flights of imagination in recent years (see my two-volume novel Jesus of Nazareth and the Kingdom of Weeds).

For much of the last 2,000 years of Christian history, the Book of Acts served as the backbone of efforts to understand the early growth of the Jesus movement. Biblical studies in the last decades offer a broader understanding of the development of the movement. The important book After Jesus Before Christianity by Brandon Scott has provided immeasurable benefit to me in grasping more clearly what happened in those opening decades after Jesus' death. Scott's book offers another perspective, one much more carefully nuanced than the Book of Acts. Acts gives a laudatory sketch of the opening ministry of Peter and an extended attention to Paul's work as he walked and preached in large portions of the Roman Empire.

Scott's book, along with other fascinating studies, especially Dominic Crossan's extensive work the Birth of Christianity provide a much more human, comprehensive picture of the early Jesus movement after that first Easter event and beyond.

Brandon Scott and his co-authors of the *After Jesus* book heed cautions from Stephen Hawking. As Hawking explored the universe from his wheelchair, he reminded seekers they must always remain radically humble. As I have said in other places, final, definitive answers for any of these great questions elude us. I can try to know and love the questions.

Mary Magdalene "Sees" the Savior

Another important expression of the Jesus movement emerged in the more eastern regions of the Empire. This group tended to emphasize the life, teachings, and human service of Jesus rather than his death. The eastern movement leaders likewise had visions of Jesus, but their experiences emphasized the present rather than heaven. This eastern expression was overshadowed, but not lost, as Rome and the western region gained theological and political power. The extended influence of Mary Magdalene became a key focus of the eastern expression of the Jesus movement in the second century.

Notes

[1] Jon Dominic Crossan, *The Birth of Christianity* (New York, HarperCollins, 1989).
[2] Bass, *A People's History of Christianity*, 27.
[3] Robert Funk, *Jesus as Precursor* (California, Polebridge Press, 1994), 83.
[4] Wilder, *Theopoetic*, 20.
[5] Scott, *After Jesus Before Christianity*, 2.
[6] Ibid, 20.
[7] Ibid.

Yes, I Am a Jesus Person

Gleanings from the gospels and years of enriching study prompt me to say emphatically I am a Jesus person. I admire what I have decided Jesus desired to accomplish. I fully embrace his hope for an unbrokered relationship between a person and their connection to the sacred, the spirit, the compelling life-giving mystery at the heart of one's existence.

Jesus is a savior in the sense that his call for practice of the golden rule, revulsion at religious and political systems that dehumanize the "others," commitment to justice and compassion brings new life to all who walk in that path.

In 1994, while reading Marcus Borg's book *Meeting Jesus Again for the First Time*, I met the Jesus I had sought but missed for forty years. Thanks to Borg and other Jesus of history scholars I came to think of Jesus in two modes the pre-Easter Jesus and the post-Easter Jesus.

The pre-Easter Jesus is the man from Nazareth. His life, love, and teaching made an indelible impression on the people who came to know him as a Galilean. Pre-Easter points toward the Jesus of everyday life in Galilee until his death. A Jewish friend reading my books about Jesus says, "I never realized Jesus had a life."

The post-Easter Jesus becomes the Christ (*Anointed, Messiah*) of faith that Paul and other early believers in Jesus came to regard as the God-raised, exalted savior of the world. The post-Easter Jesus is the expression of Jesus that caught the hopes of Paul who had life changing visions and experiences he interpreted as visitations by the risen Christ. Paul's extant writings make very little of the life of Jesus. Paul's letters concentrated on the death of Jesus and its meaning for faith. A sense of the God-raised Christ to a place of eternal honor seems to be what motivated Paul and sent him preaching into the cities of the Roman Empire.

Jesus of Nazareth died on a Roman cross. Jesus the Christ of faith, never died. He lives on in the faith, the imagination, and energy of millions for the past twenty centuries.

Here again Isaac Newton helps me: Energy is neither created nor lost. Energy can be reconfigured but never goes away. All lifeforms are energy and light. Jesus of Nazareth then as energy and light still exists if in a different form like the energy of all who have lived before us. We are infused with the energy that infused Jesus. How then does the never-lost energy of the ever-living Jesus shape our lives today? More to come.

Jesus the Christ of faith, never died.

I am learning that all life forms connect genetically. We are one with all creation from when we began in the bottom of the ocean millions of years ago. Thus, I am electrically, genetically connected to Jesus just as I am to Julius Caesar and Adolf Hitler. The existential question is always: to what energy strain do I respond, Jesus gene or Hitler gene? To the best of my ability, I deeply desire to let Jesus' Life-force have sway along with those of Moses, Jeremiah, St. Francis, Mother Theresa, Eleanor Roosevelt, Eloise Allen, Dorothy Cook, and Jimmy Carter for starters. I gratefully embrace what I understand of and about Jesus. I have an existential relationship with Jesus of Nazareth and the manifested Jesus of the twenty-first century.

My faith journey for the last 30 years has focused on Jesus of Nazareth, the pre-Easter Jesus. He concentrated his energies and ministry on the hurting people of the Galilean villages as they suffered under Roman military occupation. As Jesus' teaching ministry unfolded, he evidently began to look with greater concern at the Jerusalem temple system, underscoring his connection with the plea for justice of some of the Hebrew prophets. I have already said I do not believe that Jesus is the savior of the world. He was a man extraordinarily connected with God, a man full of God. It is this Jesus of Nazareth, this godly, motivated servant in whom I locate faith, genetic and never-lost energy connections.

I Am a Meeting Jesus Again For the First Time Person

Marcus Borg in several places lays out his understanding of Jesus of Nazareth, who went about doing good:

- Jesus was thoroughly Jewish: he was born, lived, and died as a Jew of the Roman/Herodian era.

- He sought to revitalize the Jewish traditions of his own time.

- Jesus was an extraordinary person. He inspired a deep devotion among those who knew him and walked most closely with him. He fired their hopes, energies, courage, and imagination.

- Jesus was a spirit person. He was full of God. He mediated the sacred. He walked with and lived in God. He went through "thin" places in his relationship with the Holy.

- Jesus was a teacher of wisdom, wisdom that was often subversive to the accepted social order. He was the master of the parable and aphorism. Many contemporary scholars say the parables come closest to the authentic voice of the historic Jesus. He was a social prophet in the mold of the Hebrew prophets, especially Hosea and Amos.

- He challenged the social order. The religious authorities were wary of him along with any who might upset the tenuous balance of power between them and the Romans. He despaired of the elitism of his time.

• Jesus morphed into a movement founder. The movement he fostered sought to revitalize the Jewishness of his time. The Jesus movement eventually became the Christian church over the next two centuries after the cross/Easter event.[1]

Jesus of Nazareth did not make messianic claims for himself; he always pointed everyone to Adonai. The messianic claims rose from the letters of Paul to the Jesus groups he founded and/or nurtured. Beginning a few years after Paul's death, the gospels, especially the gospel of John, gathered up the evolving theological foundations for Jesus' exalted place.

Throughout those seminal years of the development of the Jesus movement, a more elaborate Christology developed from his devoted followers after the crucifixion. The divinity with which the Christian "fathers" imbued Jesus in the second and third centuries CE set in stone the veneration of Jesus as the universal savior. In those formative centuries, the locus of the movement shifted from Galilee to Jerusalem to Rome. The divine Jesus found increasingly firm footing in the cosmovision of the non-Jewish, population of the Roman Empire.

> *The religious world into which Jesus came was a world dominated by the law and the tradition of the fathers. The received world of Judean religion in antiquity was programmed to guard the deposit of tradition delivered to Moses and the prophets, and to preserve this tradition against the day when God would restore his people to their rightful place within the economy of world history. In the meantime, God was taken to have withdrawn into the confines of sacred scripture and it's interpretation by the fathers, into the temple, and it's cultus, into the latter days surrogate, the synagogue, and into those customs which overly set the people of*

God off from the rest of humanity. Within these confines Israel was to await by faithful and patient observance of the law, the renewal of the ancient glory. The fullness of the glory would come, it was widely anticipated, in the near future.[2]

Jesus of Nazareth, the Spirit man full of the Other, the Holy beckons me. I connect genetically and spiritually with this Jesus.

Notes

[1] Marcus Borg, *Meeting Jesus Again for the First Time* (New York, Harper and Row, 1994), 20-39.

[2] Funk, *Jesus as Precursor*, 60.

I Am a Faithing Non-theist Cumulative Christian Tradition of the 21st Century Person

Do I regard myself as a Christian in the twenty-first century? Yes, emphatically yes! I archive as important echoes the sacerdotal myths about God and the deity of Jesus the movement formulated. I seek to penetrate the myths to find a semblance of the man, the one to whom I can relate.

Traditions have a mundane history. One can affix a date to a tradition. The traditions surrounding Jesus of Nazareth are rooted in a time and place. Accepting these traditions into my life as meaningful, transforming experiences is an exercise of faithing. Traditions can be evaluated. Faithing is intensely unverifiable, personal, beyond verification. So, I embrace my non-theist cumulative Christian tradition as an experience of faithing.

Here, then I rely on the concept I have previously spotlighted, the "cumulative Christian tradition" as offered by the late Professor Cantwell Smith of Harvard.[1]

I choose to frame my life in and around the cumulative Christian tradition. The tradition is rooted in the historic life of the young Galilean shaman who grew up in the tiny village of Nazareth in what we have calculated to be in the twenties of the Common Era. The secular history of his time paid no attention to him. His story as noted by traditional history begins after he died, according to tradition, by crucifixion. Mundane history about Jesus in his time is nonexistent. At that history-less point, the cumulative Christian tradition takes over.

Cumulative says, in this instance, what we value and preserve about Jesus constantly accumulated as the decades and centuries rolled by. From Jesus' well-lived life of service to the least of those, cut short by a Roman cross, a vast Christian tradition has accumulated over the past two thousand years.

The actual story, the mundane history of Jesus' daily life, is unknown. We do not have history; we have tradition. To be sure, every life is a combination of fact and tradition. The difference between the facts and tradition of my life are of little consequence. For Jesus, that equation is huge and far reaching. The fact and tradition around Jesus have fostered a world religion with vast historically validated traditions that have shaped the lives of billions of humans for centuries. Kingdoms, nations, philosophies, wars, and magnificent works of compassion have risen and fallen, not because of Jesus of Nazareth, but because of the cumulative Christian tradition we humans have believed, adopted, practiced and preserved.

✤

From what I think I know, from what I think I feel, my faithing persuades me to identify with the man I choose as a gene-energy imbued companion to "love extravagantly, live fully and be the best that I can be."

Thus, I am a Christian living within and through the cumulative Christian tradition developed for these twenty centuries. We can give time and place to the traditions; we cannot historically verify Jesus of the four canonical gospels. From what I think I know, from what I think I feel, my faithing persuades me to identify with the man I choose as a gene-energy imbued companion to "love extravagantly, live fully and be the best that I can be."

All our religions are built on a smattering of mundane history and billowing, ever expanding human tradition. I choose the Christian tradition with the same measure of cultural ethos and choice my friends choose Hinduism, Judaism, Taoism, Native American, or unfortunately White Nationalism.

Yes, by choice and faithing I am a Jesus person. At 88, I make that affirmation with more clarity than I did at 50 or 20.

Note

[1] Smith, *The Meaning and End of Religion*, 143ff.

I Am a Hebrew Bible/Christian Testament Person

Rather than the Bible as the word from God to humanity, the Bible is clusters of peoples' earnest words about God. It is a monumental error and an affront to human reason to insist that all the Bible comes as an inerrant, verbal revelation from the storied Genesis God. Human beings in search of the intuited but unknowable mystery that yet beckons wrote the Hebrew Bible and Christian Testament. The same is true for all the world's holy books.

Note: I want to move away from outdated designations of Old and New Testaments. Those terms no longer suffice. I aim to say the Hebrew Bible and the Christian Testament.

I take the Bible seriously, just not always literally. The Bible is our all-time best selling and least read book.

Preamble: Invitation to Liberation

One's animating faithing relationship with their relationship with the Holy is larger, deeper, and more personal than allegiance to the Bible or a person. The Hebrew Bible and the Christian Testament are important resources for a faithing relationship but not final, not authoritative, and not binding.

Faith formation, never finished, provides liberation, an open road, never a dead end. Yes, this boundaryless approach carries a huge share of institutional risk but it also opens Jesus' offer of abundant life. Before our Jesus ancestors had a Bible, they were embracing Mary Magdalene's echo from Jesus to seek their full humanity. Bottom line: the Bible is not the last word on Jesus' offers of abundant life.

The Bible, a document in which I have invested 70 years of joyful study and encounter, is primarily an anthology of works of poetry and imagination with drips and drabs of mundane history as the thread to hold the narrative together.

By now you know that I grew up in the Baptist Bible-dominated southern culture of the 1950s. That culture initially shaped my life far more than God and Jesus. Religion, church, Bible, and daily practice are all filtered through southern culture. Human beings create culture. Thus, southern humans had far more to do with my religious formation than all the Bible study and preaching combined. It has taken me a long time to sort through that milieu to forge a reasonable and motivating spiritual life. At 88, I think I'm getting there. If you have read this far, you have felt my personal process from the confines of southern ethos to a much more liberated experience with mystery.

Baptists of the south declared they were people of the book, the Bible. Southern Baptist Convention adherents worshiped and divided over the Bible. For the past half century, Southern Baptists leaders have fought a rearguard battle to maintain a literalist approach to the ancient disparate writings.

I know now our understanding and appreciation of this book bordered on the shameful. In numerous ways our culturally myopic approach to the Bible formed a prison around our minds. The fresh air of an ongoing, even limited, experience with life's beckoning mysteries eluded us. That narrow approach to the Bible governed our science, education, social life, racial relations, and politics. The choking confinement of the Bible was not the fault of the Bible. The jailors were those who held places of authority, who were too bound by a retreating ethos to dig out and give us the keys to spiritual daylight. Too many people still live in that prison from which they preach a toxic message.

Essentially since 1979, Linda and I have lived outside the deep south. I came to revel in the political, cultural, religious, and theological openness of our mid-Atlantic culture. In recent months,

Linda's Alzheimer's disease has made it more productive for us to move to Gainesville, Georgia. We have been warmly welcomed. So far in this boomtown, rife with technological savvy, I suffer from what I experience: a largely closed political and theological perspective. Fortunately, I am regularly connecting with an invigorating band of being-liberated *fringers*.

We live in layers, passing between the cultures we create
Crossing between worlds, we only recognize
When we leave them behind.[1]
   —Steven Charleston

I find constant adventure as I encounter the teaching, wisdom, myths, people, and history in this library, this very human anthology we have come to commonly call the Holy Bible. This newness, the humanness, has come rolling along to me in the past 30 or 40 years. I have sought to find myself in the texts as mirrors enabling me to look at myself and us maybe again for the first time. Earnest, seeking, scared, courageous, honest, and woefully duplicitous biblical human characters come straight from central casting. The ageless psalms act as a complaint box aimed at Adonai with management suggestions and pervasive embrace of steadfast love. The prophets' calls for justice resound in every generation. Poetry sings through on wings of celestial wonder.

Thus, let's nail it down: all the documents in the Hebrew and Christian scripture come from people seeking a genuine relationship with what they sensed was the Beyond, their words *about* rather than *from* God.

The Hebrew Bible

Some pieces of Hebrew scripture reach far back to the campfires of our seeking polytheistic ancestors. All scripture writers put words in the mouths of YHWH/Adonai and Jesus, both uplifting and harsh. Especially the books of Hebrew scripture have gone through numerous edits putting words in YHWH's mouth before arriving at what we generally have today. By any measure, the Hebrew Bible evolved over at least a thousand years with stories and classic myths reaching back much further.

Professor Jacob Wright (*Why the Bible Began*) says scribes of the defeated Israelite Northern Kingdom (722 BCE) and Southern Kingdom (586 BCE) rewrote then current palace histories of Israel and Judah to provide guidance to the Jewish people in their catastrophic defeats.[2] For five hundred years, the two small kingdoms had survived constant onslaughts by imperial powers. The people of Israel and Judah depended on kings to lead their nations and embody YHWH's presence among them. With kings and kingdoms wiped away (permanently), as tumultuous centuries rolled by, the surviving Israelites would either create a new self-understanding or they would be swallowed up by relentless storms of change. Dr. Wright makes the compelling case that the skillful remastering of the Torah, Books of Kings, Prophets, and Psalms offered grist that enabled the Jews to create a "peoplehood" as they were forced to live in dispersion throughout the world without a kingdom.[3]

The Christian Testament

Note: I have drawn heavily from Dr. Karen King's The Gospel of Mary Magdalene on early Christian history and Testament, especially her conversation about the "Master Story."[4]

Disparate writings appeared early, especially letters addressing the concerns of scattered Jesus communities. Partial collections allegedly containing Jesus' sayings and narratives interpreting the death and resurrection of Jesus and oral practices framed the lives of early, scattered, often illiterate Christians. Preaching, teaching, and rituals of table fellowship and baptism were the core of the first and second century Christian experience. What few written documents the groups had or knew about had served at most as supplemental guides to preaching and developing ritual practice.

History is written by the winners. With that truism in mind, evidence is compelling that among the Jesus movement, dissenting voices were steadily, relentlessly suppressed. Christian Testament scholars theorize we have lost 85 percent of Christian literature from the first two centuries and that includes only the literature we know something about.[5] Part of the loss was inevitable because of ignorance or the ravages of time. The writings of an unknown number were destroyed by powerful, prevailing male movement leaders. We must be careful that we don't suppose it is possible to reconstruct the whole of early Christian history and practice. From the few texts that remain our picture will always be partial not only because so much is lost but because early Christian practices were so little tied to durable writing.

The Christian Testament had at least two aims: celebrate and affirm the crucified Jesus as God's anointed and to deal with controversies that arose among the aborning and scattered Jesus groups. The seven undisputed letters of Paul (1 Thessalonians, Galatians, Philippians, 1 & 2 Corinthians, Philemon, Romans) to Jesus groups addressed the relationship of Jesus to traditional Judaism, circumcision, Jewish food laws, the literal or metaphorical resurrection of Jesus, spiritual gifts, and ecclesiastical lines of authority.

It is important always to remember that the first Jesus "clubs" had no Christian Testament, no Nicene or Apostles' Creed, no commonly established church order or chain of authority, no church buildings, and no single understanding of Jesus. All the elements we might consider to be essential to define Christianity did not yet exist and/or were in their earliest stages of development.

Far from being starting points, the Christian Testament and creeds were the *end* products of those first, second, and third century CE debates and disputes. These early literary efforts represent the distillation of experience and experimentation and not a small amount of strife and struggle.

The Master Story

As I described earlier, Professor Karen King of Harvard and other scholars say the Christian "Master Story" emerged in the Pauline/Rome influenced western regions of the Roman Empire. That "Master Story" prevails as the dominant orthodoxy into the twenty-first century.[6]

The "Master Story" asserts that an unbroken chain stretching from Jesus to the apostles and on to their successors and the church elders, ministers, priests, and bishops guaranteed unity and uniformity of Christian belief and practice. The correct form of this belief and practice is called orthodoxy. It is inscribed in the Christian Testament canon, the Nicene Creed, and reenacted in the ritual performances of baptism, the Lord's Supper/Eucharist, and clergy ordination.

But what happens if we tell the story differently, drawn from an expanding trove of likewise early second and third century documents? What if the beginning was a time of grappling and creative diversity? What if the meaning of the gospel was not clear and Christians struggled to understand who Jesus was and what his cruel death might mean? What if there was no unity and conformity at the beginning, rather roiling with different views and experiences?

Professor King insists that the "Master Story" is poor history; incomplete and noticeably slanted. The roles of women, for example are almost completely erased from view. In the "Master Story," the male Jesus selects male disciples who pass on traditions to male bishops. Yet we know in the early centuries and throughout Christian history women have played prominent roles as apostles, teachers, preachers and prophets.

The triumph of Nicene orthodoxy declared other views of Christianity heretical. That historic tragedy began to change dramatically with the discovery of the Nag Hammadi Library in 1946. These documents, buried in a huge earthen jar for fifteen centuries in an Egyptian hillside, provide a wealth of primary works that illustrate the diverse character of early Christianity. Pauline theology is but one side of a story about early followers of Jesus working out what it means to be a Christian in a world where Jews and gentiles shared meals together. We need to understand that theological diversity, not consensus, marked the early Jesus movement. Not enforced orthodoxy, the norm was earnest experimentation and seeking enriched by poetry and imagination. Vital faithing in the twenty-first century depends on that measure of resilient liberation.

Important Clues from Chronology

Marcus Borg in *Evolution of the Word* presents the writings of the Christian canon in the historic chronological order in which he proposes they were written.[7] This listing provides a perspective on how the Jesus movement, developed from Jesus in the 30s CE into the late second century CE. In Borg's prescient book, Paul's First Thessalonians letter is the earliest book of the canon, not Matthew. That letter from the 50s CE gives the earliest extant description of Jesus as Christ, not as in Matthew. The gospel *reflects* rather than *introduces* Jesus as Christ. Thus, unlike the Hebrew Bible, the Christian canon has a much shorter evolution from about 50 CE to 180 CE.

The developing Jesus movement, becoming the Christian church, used some of the earlier documents in worship and teaching. The canon did not become official dogma until 397 CE when the Bishops' Council of Hippo ratified the list we use today. The earliest known listing of the full canon dates from 367 CE. Marcion (early second century) was among the initial movement leaders to issue a partial list. He also helped revive Paul's letters that had fallen into suspicion and disuse.

With the small book of 2 Peter (120 to 150 CE), written in the long-dead apostle's name, the Christian Testament was unofficially but practically closed as the Jesus movement expanded into its third century.

We need to note that those opening decades saw the writing of many documents dealing with a wide range of topics relating to Jesus and the movement. Only twenty-seven of that huge potpourri made it into the canon.

The Bible, like any complex body of work, yields itself more fully to serious study. Biblical scholars teach us to read the biblical stories forward rather than backward, starting where the story starts. Marcus Borg consistently urges the reader to get "their then" before we jump to "our now."[8]

One can find anything or prove any point one chooses in the Bible by lifting snatches of scripture. For instance, in some pieces Jesus seems to say ask for anything and you will get it. In other accounts, Jesus says if you want to keep your life, give it away. Coming to the broader meaning of scripture requires the seeker to look for the larger context, the linguistic and/or historic setting of the passage. It is invariably risky to build a large system on a few snatches of one-liners. Always when facing any difficult question in scripture try to ask what does love call for in this situation?

To get inside a particular passage in Hebrew or Christian scripture, I try to dig deeper into the passage. Dating documents is an invaluable clue to the larger context. Honest, broad-minded commentaries abound on all aspects of the Bible. They are also typically friendly to use. Wikipedia is handy with quick research articles and usually dependable.

Make a genuine effort to discern what may be an important spiritual mandate and what might simply be advice offered to address first century cultural concerns. For instance, the way a woman wears her hair to a worship service is not important. Treating everyone with respect is important.

I try to get acquainted with biblical characters to see if we can talk with each other and feel their hopes and fears. I ask what were their issues that prompted action in a certain direction? Always make every effort for love to serve as the ultimate filter, not just the local culture or one's prejudice.

The Charter Myth

I have come to see the Christian Testament as the "Charter Myth" of the developing Jesus movement (from 30 CE) that gradually became institutionalized as the Christian church (into the third century CE).

By charter I mean the Christian Testament both reflects and gives form to the identifiable, historic traditions that slowly, inexorably grew from the first Easter into the third century.

By myth I mean the Christian Testament embraces the intangible, spiritual hopes, dreams, fantasies, poetry, and fertile imaginations of those early followers of Jesus. Myth frames the flights of imagination the early writers employed to tell their story of devotion to Jesus as the unique, raised son of God. The myths also aim to give Jesus status in the Empire's religious culture. The birth narratives in Matthew and Luke are beautiful myths. Jesus' temptation narratives, Jesus walking on water, bringing Lazarus out of his grave, and the gorgeous resurrection stories are myths. A myth conveys a truth or a hope beyond historicity.

The Declaration of Independence can be regarded as our national Charter Myth. Get serious with the Bible. You will be delighted and enriched.

For Jewish and Christian people, the Bible is our book, light on the pathways of everyday life. It is an enduring treasure from our ancestors as they sought their ways to God. Inspired, spiritually eager men and a few women like you and me wrote what has become our collected search for life's meaning. Let us pause and thank them for their grand, courageous adventure into Mystery.

Notes

[1] Charleston, *Spirit Wheel*, 157.
[2] Jacob L. Wright, *Why the Bible Began*, 12ff.
[3] Ibid.,12.
[4] King, *The Gospel of Mary Magdalene*, 155-190.
[5] Ibid., 165.
[6] Ibid., 159.
[7] Marcus Borg, *Evolution of the Word* (New York, HarperCollins, 2012).
[8] Ibid., 5.

I Am an Ecclesia, Local Jesus Club, Person

Ecclesia is a charming Greek word meaning an assembly of people gathered for a particular purpose. The word comes from ancient Athens as citizens, all male and open only to certain classes, gathered periodically to deal with the politics and needs of the city. Once in session, regardless of class, they voted democratically.

The Jesus *ecclesia* evolved from Roman society. Roman public life reflected peoples' enduring need for community, friendship, collective help in times of trouble, and focused action to deal with troublesome civic issues. People throughout much of the Empire gathered in *ecclesiae*, that is clubs, associations, guilds, and quasi political parties. The towns' clubs usually met in homes or public squares since rarely did they have their own meeting halls. Food was integral to club meetings. Everyone had a say in the gatherings.

The Jesus people naturally replicated the way their neighbors functioned socially. The established local societies understood the Jesus groups likewise as clubs, guilds, collections of neighbors meeting to talk about their new god, Jesus. They met in homes or public spaces. Followers of Jesus, at first only a handful of believers in a town, needed the same elements of community, association, and identity realized in the larger culture.

Most Roman towns and cities had some variation of basilicas where law courts met. These rectangular buildings could also be used for larger public gatherings and stage productions. The earliest known Christian church structures date from the middle to the late third century. These early structures typically reflected the architecture of Roman basilicas with long, high-ceilinged naves flanked by two aisles. Larger church buildings also came to be called basilicas.

Of the ten known oldest church structures, seven are still in use. The other three lie in ruins.

In time, movement leaders emerged who picked up on the way Rome governed its far-flung colonies. Roman governors were often called bishops (overseers), so church leaders adopted that nomenclature for their leaders. Rome called its territories dioceses, hence Christian bishops governed areas that were likewise dubbed dioceses. The Pontifex Maximus served as the titular leader of Roman state religion. Along the way, the bishop of Rome (who became the pope) appropriated the title Pontifex Maximus.

I am an *ecclesia* person. I need a faith community: a human garden in which I can grow, find comfort in times of stress, laced through with the freedom, and even the encouragement, to push to the outer limits of my own spiritual universe. The church of my choice, with all its warts, is the unique institution that aims to embrace, without regard to race, every child, adult, single, married, divorced, gay, straight, transgender, and like all of us, quite flawed.

My beloved United Church of Christ in Bethesda, Maryland says, "Whoever you are and wherever you are on life's journey, you are welcome here." Our denomination practices what it preaches. The United Church Christ was the first denomination to ordain gay women and men for church leadership. Our minister and music director are openly gay men with grand gifts of leadership and spirit. I have joyfully conducted several same sex weddings. I conducted a graveside service for an aborted fetus who had died in his mother's womb when the parents' home church cast them out.

My earliest childhood memory harks back to the moment when I was in a young children's Sunday school class. As a fourth-grade boy coming along in Portsmouth, Virginia during World War II, I found a neighborhood church to attend while my parents dealt with war-related work and stress. As a teenager, our local church held sway as the center of my social life. In a church Sunday evening training class I first realized I could think and talk on my feet.

I offer heartfelt appreciation for the congregations that nurtured me growing up: Lithonia Baptist Church; Clarkston Baptist Church; Seventh and James Baptist Church; First Baptist Church, Arlington, Texas; and Columbia Baptist Church.

I express my deepest gratitude for the congregations that allowed me to partner with them as pastor beginning in 1964: First Baptist Church, Vienna, Georgia; First Baptist Church, Calhoun, Georgia; Mayfield Road Baptist Church, Arlington, Texas; and especially Briggs Baptist Church, Bethesda, Maryland from 1992 until 2006. In 2006, I had the opportunity along with our Briggs congregation to become part of the next-door Westmoreland Congregational United Church of Christ in Bethesda, Maryland.

I concluded my pastoral time at the Westmoreland Church as interim pastor when the church called my great friend Tim Tutt as pastor. Still now, I am yet an *ecclesia* person. To provide top-notch care for Linda's illness, we moved back to Georgia in the spring of 2024. We promptly connected with the First Baptist Church of Gainesville, Georgia where we have been graciously welcomed. I have also found warm friends in the city's Grace Episcopal Church and other church-related groups.

Bishop John Shelby Spong in his last book *Unbelievable* provides me with an eloquent and evocative conclusion:

Christianity is called to be a community of self-conscious people who have transcended the boundaries that divide human beings from another. It is also called to be a community of people committed to a journey into the future going beyond even the cloud of unknowing as a fourteenth century mystic termed it

Christianity is charged with the task of creating a place in which all can hear about and contemplate the meaning of life and thus be introduced to that which is ultimately real. Such a community of believing will of necessity give up any role in judgment, sacrifice all claims to possess the truth in any concrete form and refrain from ever again hiding a documented evil under the guise of sacred scripture

Christianity must be a place in which human oneness is practiced and where human engagement with that which is eternal can be practiced. This is finally what Christianity must come to mean. I welcome the Christianity to which this vision beckons me I bear witness to the faith that leads me and the whole world to love wastefully, to live fully, and be all that we can be.[1]

"Blest be the tie" that gently, lovingly enfolds us.

Note

[1] Spong, *Unbelievable*, 287.

The Author

Robert (Bob) Maddox is the oldest of four sons born in 1937 to Robert and Virginia Maddox of Atlanta, Georgia. Bob was baptized in the Lithonia (Georgia) Baptist Church at age thirteen. He is a graduate of Clarkston High School, Baylor University, Southwestern Baptist Seminary and Candler School of Theology, Emory University. In addition to pastorates in Texas, Georgia, and Maryland he was a White House speechwriter to President Jimmy Carter and Executive Director of Americans United for the Separation of Church and State and Editor of the *Capital Baptist* of the District of Columbia Baptist Convention. He is the author of numerous articles and editorials, eight adult Sunday School Bible studies and seven books including a two-volume novel *Jesus of Nazareth and the Kingdom of Weeds*.

In 1959, Bob and Linda Cook from Thomaston, Georgia, were married. They have three children and five grandchildren. Linda and Bob have recently moved to Phoenix on Lake Lanier, a senior adult community, in Gainesville, Georgia.

Selected Bibliography

Bass, Diana Butler. Christianity for *The Rest of Us; A Peoples History of Christianity*. Harper Collins, 2009.

Borg, Marcus. *Evolution of the Word*. Harper One, 2012.

Borg, Marcus. *Meeting Jesus Again for the First Time*. Harper One, 1994.

Brown, Raymond. *The Birth of the Messiah*. Doubleday, 1977

Brown, Raymond. *The Death of the Messiah*. Doubleday, 1994

Cantwell Smith, Wilfred. *The Meaning and End of Religion*. Princeton University Press, 1972.

Charleston, Steven. *Spirit Wheel: Meditations from an Indigenous Elder*. Broadleaf Books, 2023.

Charleston, Steven. *Ladder to the Light: An Indigenous Elder's Meditations on Hope and Courage*. Broadleaf Books, 2021.

Crossan, Jon Dominic. *The Birth of Christianity*. Harper Collins, 1989.

Crossan, Jon Dominic. *Who Killed Jesus*. Harper San Francisco, 1995

Crossan, Jon Dominic. *The Greatest Prayer*. Harper One, 2011

Crossan, Jon Dominic and Marcus Borg. *The Last Week*. Harper San Francisco, 2006.

Crossan, Jon Dominic. *The Birth of Christianity*. Harper Collins, 1998.

Cox, Brian and Jeff Forshaw. *Black Holes*. Harper Collins Publishers, 2022.

Cupit, Don. Numerous readings.

Eagleman, David. *Incognito*. Cannongate, 2011.

Funk, Robert. *Jesus as Precursor*. Polebridge Press, 1994.

Geering, Lloyd. Numerous readings.

Hakim, Joy. *Story of Science: Aristotle, Isaac Newton, Einstein*. Smithsonian Books, 2007.

Harari, Uvari Noah. *Sapiens*. HarperCollins, 2018.

Hawking, Stephen. *A Brief History of Time*. Bantam Books, 1988.

Higginbotham, Stuart. *The Heart of a Calling*. Crossroad Publishing Company. 2021.

Isaacson, Walter. *Einstein*. Simon & Schuster, 2017.

Isaacson, Walter. *Leonardo Da Vinci*. Simon & Schuster, 2017.

King, Karen. *The Gospel of Mary Magdalene*. Polebridge Press, 2003.

Maddox, Robert L. *Jesus of Nazareth and the Kingdom of Weeds: A Novel*. Nurturing Faith, 2020

Maddox, Robert L. *A Faith Journey: No Boundaries, No Conclusions*. Nurturing Faith, 2018.

Pagels, Elaine. *The Origin of Satan*. Penguin Press, 1995.

Popova, Maria. *The Universe in Verse*. Storey Publishing, 2024.

Readings from The Nag Hammadi Library.

Reston, James. *Galileo*. HarperCollins, 1994.

Rutherford, Adam. *Humanimal*. Weldenfield & Nicoloson, 2018.

Scott, Brandon. *After Jesus to Christianity*. HarperCollins, 2021.

Scott, Brandon. *Hear then the Parables*. Fortress Press, 1990.

Smith, Dennis E. & Tyson, Joseph B. *Acts and Christian Beginnings*. Polebridge, 2013.

Spong, John Shelby. *Unbelievable*. Harper Collins, 2018.

Tonelli, Guido. *Genesis*. Picador Books, 2019.

Wilder, Amos. *Theopoetic*. Wipf & Stock, 1972.

Wilder, Amos. *Theology and the Religious Imagination*. Wipf and Stock, 1976.

Wright, Jacob. *Why the Bible Began*. Cambridge University Press, 2023.

www.ingramcontent.com/pod-product-compliance
Lightning Source LLC
Chambersburg PA
CBHW071007160426
43193CB00012B/1953